THE PERFECT STRANGER

THE
PERFECT
STRANGER

The Truth About Mothers and Nannies

Lucy Kaylin

BLOOMSBURY

At the interviewees' request, some names and
identifying details have been changed.

Published by Bloomsbury USA, New York
Distributed to the trade by Holtzbrinck Publishers

All papers used by Bloomsbury USA are natural, recyclable products made
from wood grown in well-managed forests. The manufacturing processes con-
form to the environmental regulations of the country of origin.

LIBRARY OF CONGRESS CATALOGING-IN-PUBLICATION DATA
HAS BEEN APPLIED FOR.

ISBN-10 1-58234-407-8
ISBN-13 978-1-58234-407-2

First U.S. Edition 2007

1 3 5 7 9 10 8 6 4 2

Typeset by Westchester Book Group
Printed in the United States of America by Quebecor World Fairfield

For Owen

CONTENTS

THE GREAT DEBATE

YOU RISE IN the early morning half-light and move stealthily from your bed so as not to wake your husband. You go past the hushed rooms in which the children lie sprawled in sleep, watched over by a hundred pairs of impassive button eyes. Then it's on to the shower, where you'll wash away the cozy aroma, the smelly warmth of home.

Ready for phase two in your terry-cloth turban, you stare into the mirror and start applying color, drawing lines around your eyes—in effect putting on your day mask: a more sharply articulated, expressive, aggressive you. The children are awake and drifting around now, quietly bleating their breakfast wish list and foggily regarding your busy, curiously transforming rituals that involve mean little tools like metal files and tweezers. The hair dryer screams as your little girl, crowding you about the hips, reaches for a tube of lotion you're about to use—a tantalizing artifact of that cluttered, purpose-driven foreign land of adulthood. You tell her to leave it alone, but she can't—knowing negative attention beats no attention at all. So she knocks the cap down the drain and squirts out a full third of the overpriced contents. And suddenly you understand that expression about blood boiling—you know what that feels like, to be so trapped in emotions that all you can do is bark something hurtful, laced with sarcasm your daughter doesn't even understand, something you'll instantly regret. Ashamed but pressed for time, you retreat to your room and don the workplace gear: the skirt, the belt, the hard, shiny shoes that will punctuate your every move with a *clack*.

Around this time the doorbell rings, signaling the changing of the guard. And there she is, carrying a takeout cup of tea— the tag on a string draped over the side—and a couple of warm muffins in a sack for the kids. Fragrant, ample of bosom, put together. Awake now for two hours at least, time enough to get here from a distant and very different neighborhood, she's in step with the day, in control, ready for anything. The children streak toward her and grab her legs, crowding her about the hips. And as she moves through the house, the kids trailing behind, asking for Cheerios/raisins/juice (for they know there's a very good chance that she can actually meet their needs; that's why she's here), she glances left and right, assessing all that must be done. Not just the beds to make and the littered, gummy surfaces to wipe down, but the jazzed toddlers who need settling and focusing, and the irritable mother who must be transitioned out of the scene intact so that the day can officially get under way. It is time now for you to move on, feeling good about the arrangement you have made and confident that the woman you have chosen to care for your children is as perfect as she seems. And is in no way a threat to your role as Mom.

Then you head for the door with newspaper and keys, a study in shades of black and gray. At which point, as if on cue, your son races toward you with butter-smeared paws and a board book about a duck family that he'd like you to read to him. What could be better? What could be more delicious than taking a little time out for that? But the skirt is expensive and the meeting is in an hour—what choice have you got but to turn him away?

At the door you make one final, flailing play for control before relinquishing it entirely, launching a fusillade of trivial instructions about playdates and snacks and no TV (some chance). And as you go out with a pasting of kisses that effectively seals off this part of the day, the nanny settles in, slipping off her street shoes and into the soft-soled ones she keeps here, up on a shelf, in a discreet corner of the closet in the hall.

She takes over. You're out the door, and she's in control.

Hiring a stranger to help you raise your kids—funny how an act designed to simplify your life can wind up being the trickiest, most controversial thing you'll ever do. And plenty of us are doing it. A onetime luxury enjoyed by the idle rich— conjuring images of a cosseted baby Churchill in an unimaginable day when kids were seen and not heard, brought round to their folks for a glimpse and a peck after the bath by a servant in a starchy uniform—nannies have become commonplace in households powered by two incomes. Rife as the profession is with undocumented workers—illegal aliens, in other words—it is impossible to know exactly how commonplace, although informed estimates have it that as many as a million women are currently working as nannies in the United States.

For most of us who suddenly find ourselves in the curious position of household employer, there's nothing fancy about this arrangement in the least. On the contrary, it's something sweaty and cobbled together, a solution not even remotely thought through, born of a naked need for another set of hands—someone to bail the boat while we row.

But okay, let's be honest. If it were merely a question of making the rent—were money that tight and options that few—many of us would have our children in day care, shuttling them to a place where they'd share the caregiver with several other children at a fraction of the cost. No, the new nanny class, though in the broadest sense middle class (by no means vixenish and pampered in the *Nanny Diaries* sense), is largely comprised of mothers with that crippling affliction: a modicum of choice. Many of us have chosen, for instance, to live in one of America's first or second cities, from Los Angeles to Atlanta, if not an equally appealing amenities-rich suburb; to some, it's simply a more stimulating life. But its knee-buckling cost might well require both you and your husband to hold down jobs. How convenient, considering you always wanted a career in the first place—to do your own thing, to make your own money. You are, in your bones, a working person.

As the phenomenon of working mothers grows widespread, so does our ambivalence about it—requiring, as it does, that we leave our kids in the care of a proxy. For all the intimacy and in-home comforts that one-on-one arrangement can provide, the essential fraudulence of installing someone momlike in your home so that you can go off and do something else isn't in any way easy to reconcile. And the leap of faith it requires can make you crazy.

How could it not? You spend nine months physically enmeshed with this new life; you are its keeper in the most literal sense, and you've never cared more about anything. Catch a belch of bus exhaust and you're on the phone to the obstetrician—*Did I just endanger my baby?* Visit your sister the cat lover and suffer a string of sleepless nights about the toxoplasmosis you surely contracted when Mr. Boots curled up on your lap with imperceptible traces of feces between the pads of his paws. And what of all that roll-on deodorant and sunblock you've been applying with abandon (none of which has been proven to produce three-headed babies, by the way). *Why not just inject the fetus with poison?*

Underscoring the fragility, the preciousness of it all, those high-risk nine months might well have been preceded by years of planning and trying, during which one's desire for a child is forged into something excruciatingly acute. *I'd dump it all for a kid,* you vow on those desperate nights when the hugely complicating prospect of parenthood masquerades as some sort of solution. Suddenly sex is no longer sex—it's a mad grab for purchase on the sheerest cliff, the balance of your life, that perilous thing you've somehow got to master.

So the baby arrives and it's all true: still awed by the fact that you survived the delivery, you have never felt more alive. You're an animal—even better, a mighty machine (as your son's insufferable video series about earth movers and the like would have it)—capable of miracles, and more efficient in its purpose than anything the corporate world could ever dream up. Nothing—not your apartment, your cat, your vintage hat collection, your diary—has ever been more fundamentally, more mystically yours, resembling you in appearance and affect. This is your spawn, your project, your life, in thoroughly mind-blowing fashion. And then in about a week or two, as real life pulls back into view, you begin to make plans for handing him off.

What's interesting about motherhood in America in the twenty-first century is that while raising children is an act as intensely public as it's ever been—perhaps even more so, given a fevered, media-driven consumerist dimension that creates the illusion of a shared experience (when we're all using the same strollers and sippy cups, watching the same shows, logging on to the same educational Web sites, and paging through the same unremittingly cheerful kid magazines full to bursting with events and tips and crafts that mother and child can do together, how could we feel alone?)—one senses vast uncertainty and private desperation all around. We're eyeing one another, surreptitiously checking out the way others do things, feeling the full range of emotions from envy to smugness, depending on the state of our self-esteem that day. There is a silly but strong temptation to take it personally when another mother makes a distinctly different choice about how to raise her children, whom she loves just as much as you love your own.

As one mother astutely put it to me, the taboo topic in polite conversation isn't politics or religion anymore—it's parenting. I will never forget sitting outside my daughter's dance class one day with a stay-at-home mom friend whose daughter was in the class as well. It was our custom to chat avidly about matters light and dark during these periods of waiting for our girls to finish, and one day I told her about the book I was going to write concerning the unique relationship we forge with these women whose job it is to care for and love our children. At which point my friend deadpanned, "Yes, but it's a mercenary kind of love. You have to pay for it." Her words sliced clear through to my heart; it was such a cold, cruel judgment on my choices, my life. My nanny! Someone I loved. More than that, though, she'd driven the harsh, rooting beam of a flashlight into the gulf between us, between a mother who turns her back on home to go to work versus one who's said good-bye to all that in order to make the work of home her job. It was startling, loaded. There was a clear sense of opposing camps, of battle lines drawn.

The situation is fragile, combustible; we're all a hair's breadth from a screeching, tear-stained defense of the choices we've made. Until such a moment arises, we play it as cool as we can while keeping our eyes open, clinically assessing the modus operandi of our peers and calculating the cost-benefit ratio of their choices versus ours: *She gave up a six-figure job to bake cupcakes and pour juice sixteen times a day. No, I don't know who the playdates are with this week, but I am palpably uplifted by that stride across the slick marble foyer every morning to my office, a place where I'm admired and listened to and expected to create. Besides, I get freebie tickets to things like Ringling Brothers and Disney premieres, which makes me the rainmaker in the eyes of my kids. A legitimate item for the plus column, no?* Noting the intense, frequently jaundiced interest we all seem to take in one another's approach to mothering, I'm reminded of that hilarious photo of Sophia Loren staring sidelong into the gleefully exposed bosom of an oblivious Jayne Mansfield. We've all become masters of the not-so-subtle sidelong glance.

In some sense we're adrift in ill-defined times, in no way united as a generation of women by some overtly political or evolutionary imperative that gives shape and urgent new meaning to our decisions. We certainly haven't got anything as tone-setting and life-changing as World War II, which drove hordes of formerly stay-at-home women into the workforce in munitions factories and anywhere else they might be needed as men vacated their positions and headed overseas for combat. (Hence, the birth of modern day care, a blatant necessity in a time of crisis encouraged and cultivated by that always forward-looking feminist Eleanor Roosevelt.)

On the face of it, women today are the complacent beneficiaries of The Struggle, several cycles past the great sacrifices of the seventies, wherein eschewing parenthood was taking a stand—breaking free—and redefining the sort of life that was possible for us. Although many probably never saw it this way, those at the leading edge of that movement gave up a lot in casting off coercive, prescribed notions of the roles women were allowed to play in society, but it was that important. A revolution was under way.

By the eighties the idea of sacrifice fell drastically out of fashion—the specter of childlessness not sitting well with the superwomen roaming the land in packs, wearing dark suits, floppy silk bows at their necks, commuter Reeboks, and expressions of wild-eyed competence, defiantly demonstrating that we *could* have it all, as that era's laughably fictive, reductive motto would have it. ("The warrior mom," as one friend, a former lawyer, acidly puts it: "Put on your man suit and power tie and go conquer the world with your little briefcase.") Whether or not any one sector of their lives was satisfying and fulfilling in the least seemed somehow beside the point. The juggle was all, as was the right these women had won at the end of the day, before collapsing into bed, to say that they'd somehow pulled it off.

Having descended from women drowning in the unbearable fullness of their lives, some mothers of the nineties chose to scale back, thanks to valid new options like part-time and flextime, while others took a defiant stand in choosing a wholesale retreat to the hearth (the decade's tech-stock boom playing no small part in enabling a wider array of families to even consider such an expensive option). These years saw the proliferation of the stay-at-home CEO, women who had gamely capitalized on the lessons and opportunities of liberation, pursuing fancy degrees and elite careers, only to chuck it all when the babies arrived.

Hence the roaring efficiency of the school fund-raiser, the holiday party, events that were now cochaired by erstwhile MBAs desperate to put their dormant skills to use. ("That was the most rewarding mom experience ever," a former world beater tells me about running the spring auction at her daughter's school. "I got to tell people what to do, and I got to get things done the way I wanted them done. I got to think, I got to write, I got to organize things. Isn't that a sad statement?") After decades of self-reinvention and adventurous forays into the formerly male strongholds of higher education and serious careers, many women, in effect, cycled back toward home. Only this time, unlike in their mothers' generation of the fifties and early sixties, they were ostensibly doing so by choice.

But there was a ferocity to it, to the rib-crushing embrace of Martha Stewart's dictum of do-it-yourself perfection (the task of stenciling clowns and bears on the walls of the nursery gone about feverishly, sized up and prepped for as though this were the MCATs). In such a climate, a compromise-averse outfit like La Leche League, the breast-feeding support group, found converts in some of these overachieving types for whom failure at parenthood was not an option, who looked to atone for the selfishness of the era by giving it all up, earth-mother-style, to the baby. Thus, they became tethered to their children, dedicating themselves to the task of providing the nutrition only a mother could produce. A strain of what looked like maternal fundamentalism had crept in—feminism as we knew it forcibly turned back.

Is anyone better for it? Generally what you hear is a lot of defensiveness masquerading as certitude: I cannot tell you how many hyperarticulate, option-laden women I've known, who at the slightest provocation straighten their spines and adopt that familiar tone of refined clarity as they declaim on the sacrosanct subject of "*My* child," and how the only caregiver good enough for him was of course Mommy herself, leaving those of us who'd hired help to feel as though we'd tossed ours so casually in a Dumpster. Of course, the self-satisfaction is altogether illusory. A few years back, *Harper's Index* put it rather starkly: "Percentage of employed U.S. mothers who think full-time mothers look down on them: 66. Percentage of full-time mothers who think employed mothers look down on them: 73."

You'd think after that many years of hand-wringing self-analysis and trial and error we would have come up with a fail-safe model, the approach to motherhood that yields the happiest children with the least amount of martyrdom and soul-crushing sacrifice on our part. But nothing, it seems, has been resolved. The archetypes have been laid out: selfless homebound mother versus childless woman versus frantic supermom versus some schizophrenic, on-and-off blend. There aren't a lot of variations left on this theme—only new mothers taking their shot and hoping their instincts are the right ones. Hoping they don't screw up their kids, and themselves in the process, completely.

Although each generation of women is thoroughly worked over by a fresh array of cultural forces, plenty of things never seem to change: no matter how endearingly evolved her husband, how enlightened her place of business, how open-minded she considers herself to be, almost every woman knows the brunt of the parenting resides with her. The health and well-being, the success or failure of her children, will largely be seen as a reflection of the kind of mother she is. As such, she chooses to indulge in the kind of self-enriching activities that take her out of the home for long stretches—i.e., she has a career—at her peril. And if her solution to the consequent child-care predicament is to hire a woman she barely knows to love her kid and keep him safe, clean, happy, and moving comfortably along the moral path she and her husband have marked out for him, well, heaven help her. For she is entering into one of the most potentially rich and important relationships she'll ever know, but also the most fraught. It will change her. For a time, anyway, it will rule her life.

At its most elemental, this book is a plea for absolution from the guilt, the fear, the gnawing ambivalence that comes with enlisting the help of a nanny. With choice and its happy precursor, power, comes responsibility, and I will argue that it is time to accept responsibility for having chosen to go forth, work, mix it up, make a mark, create, *and* come home to the unreal joy of a little baby who loves us, who's all ours. And if the only way we can somehow manage both is by hiring a surrogate to do the mommy stuff when we're not around, well, so be it. It's an arrangement that'll take some getting used to, to say the least, and that's what this book is all about. Enter into the relationship with care and respect, with eyes and heart open; honor it, work on it, do it right—and it may be the best thing that ever happened to you.

That's my sense of it, anyway. But where do my sisters-in-momhood stand on the issue? What, in their eyes, are the triumphs, the challenges, the humps they can't for the life of them get over? I wanted to find out; I wanted to learn where it is that we frequently go wrong, in an effort to figure out how we can all do better.

It was important to me to characterize this tricky moment in time for American mothers. Understand, though, *The Perfect Stranger* is not sociology (to wit, the oversimplified sketch of the female experience over the past five decades you read above). I didn't canvass the country in search of a geographically/economically/racially representative sample of contemporary American women. My inquiry was more impressionistic than scientific; there's a slippery, elusive quality to the information I sought, a truth that wouldn't be divined through census data and polling. Although I interviewed women from around the country, I tended to focus on the urban experience in the Northeast not only because that reflects my experience, the experience that made me want to write this book, but also because there's such a strong concentration of mothers there with careers, and such a vast pool of immigrant women who gravitate to the region knowing that a nanny job is one of the few ways available to them to gain an instant economic foothold. It's a big issue in those parts.

Needless to say, there is no sense in which I set out to write the last word on this baroque and ever-changing topic. Rather, I hoped to crystallize this curious era in which women are demonstrably freer and better equipped than ever to design their lives to their exact specifications, yet find themselves stymied, self-doubting. Why is that? I wanted to know. And how can we move past it?

At bottom, I hoped to capture in as detailed and accurate a way as I could the essence of the relationship between a mother and a nanny—the frustrations, the surprises, the intricacies of that daily dance. With its power struggles and ineffable intimacy, this uneasy union of mutual need is as potentially involved and tumultuous as a romance, from that giddy first blush, to the forging of a bond, to the comfort and grind of a relentless routine, to the awful specter of a breakup. If you are unsure about the choices you've made, that woman you've hired to supplement you in this most primal of endeavors will come to represent everything wonderful and terrible about your life now. She's your savior and your bane all at once. I wanted to capture the highs and lows, the unique paradoxes of that relationship, which, in the life of a mother, tend to be utterly unique.

Although nannies are generally less inclined to unload on this topic (particularly to a tape recorder–wielding mother), I wanted to give them a voice in these pages as well. (A note on terms: while the word "nanny" used to refer exclusively to women who lived in with a family, it has become an acceptable term for anyone in this job who is a pro, a lifer, in contrast to the fourteen-year-old gum snapper the word "babysitter" connotes.) These stoic, poker-faced, all-seeing women are rarely given the chance to vent their frustrations except with one another on park benches. If they want to keep their jobs, they have to roll with the chaos and vicissitudes of family life, with the strife and the unpredictability of a household that isn't theirs, where the customs may be abhorrent to them— where they'll find themselves elbow-deep in dirty laundry of the literal and figurative kind that's not their own. Navigating regularly around pajama-clad bosses whose personal problems are strewn about the house like the colorful plastic toys they gather up and put away a dozen times a day, they have a wide-open window onto our lives, and an opinion of this job that might shock you. I wanted to give them a chance to share their point of view.

And what about the father? Yes, he's incredibly important in the equation—a fully committed member of the family who'd happily give marrow for his kids. And yet he tends to be involved with the nanny in only the most tangential sense: an occasional writer of checks, perhaps; the guy scooting past, grabbing his coffee from the microwave. His chief role in the female drama unfolding each day in the middle of his home is that of sometime peacemaker and facilitator; he badly needs things to go well between the two of you, as hell hath no fury like a mother and nanny out of sorts with each other. For the most part, this issue is not about dads. It's about moms who have made the exceedingly bold choice to tap someone to be *them* during the day. It's the story of that boldness I wanted to tell.

Most of all, I want to fill this book with voices and anecdotes that will either prove comforting in their familiarity, refreshing in their perspective, or instructively scary in what they reveal. I very much hoped to create a sense of dialogue on a topic that never fails to raise hackles. We really aren't supposed to complain about motherhood; we're not expected to question the miracle or quibble about our luck in having found a little help. But putting your tiny children in the care of a stranger who will take their lives in her hands and, thus, yours as well? Your ambivalence is justified, your sense of being in the woods just right.

There's a world of us out there making it up as we go, rattled by the absence of game plan or precedent. Pride and self-preservation dictate that we appear confident about the kind of mother we've chosen to be, but in the private hours we're something else: overwhelmed, worried, quietly blindsided by the complexity and the potentially catastrophic repercussions. But we are all doing our best, trying to figure it out against unforeseen odds. In other words, you are not alone. That knowledge, more than anything, is what I hope you will take from this book.

TAKING THE PLUNGE

IT BEGAN AS a day like any other since Sophie was born six weeks before. At 10 a.m. I felt poleaxed by fatigue, having been roughing it with the baby since 4 a.m. In all my life as a working person, including summers cocktail-waitressing at a mob yacht club and cashiering at a Howard Johnson's just off the interstate, I'd never known such a punishing routine: the piteous dead-of-night squeak and whimper, my muttering trudge to the crib, nursing on the couch in the living room so as not to disturb my unconscious husband. And there I'd sit, gazing out the window as night turned to day and the water tower atop the apartment building across the way gradually grew visible in the predawn gloaming while the baby sucked so hard I thought I might lose a nipple. (She'd already drawn blood around week two, before I was told by some mom about a miracle nipple cream—who knew about such things?—and the fabled soothing powers of cabbage leaves, cunningly breast-shaped at that.)

Unfortunately, the arrival of a new day brought nothing in the way of change, relief, a break from the routine. My husband did what he could, jostling and goo-gooing the baby while I brushed my teeth (the luxury of a shower being out of the question) and making and wrapping a sandwich for my lunch, likely to take place a few hours later. (On my own with a screaming baby, I had neither the ingenuity nor the agility for juggling her meals and the preparation of my own.) And then around nine, my husband would kiss cheeks and walk out the door, leaving me to survey the vast wasteland of the day that lay ahead.

Having held a job every day since college, not counting a year of graduate school, I was woefully disoriented by the gaping absence of structure, but I did my best. Although as it unfolded, a typical day of maternity leave wasn't, I suspected, exactly what my husband pictured as he strode with new-dad pride and gusto up the block.

Here's how it went down: When he was safely on his way, I would strap a ludicrous contraption to my midsection, a heavily padded nursing doughnut; hoist the baby on top of the doughnut and array some key items in an arm's-reach semicircle around us on the bed: phone, remote, magazine, burp cloth, pacifier. Then we'd assume the nursing position as I proceeded to do something shameful—nurse the baby regardless of her needs—because it kept her busy and that was my only chance at peace. (Not child abuse, really, as she was always more than happy and ready to nurse.) With her mouth epoxied to me I could watch Rosie O'Donnell (still in her "Queen of Nice" phase and thus a comfort) in relative tranquility. More important, I could talk on the phone with friends from work who would keep me abreast, as it were, of the office gossip, on which I gorged myself like never before.

But this particular day was different. On this day I actually missed the last segment of *Rosie* because I had an appointment: at eleven, a woman was coming to interview for the position of my new baby's nanny.

Week six. That's a pivotal time for a new mom, especially if her natural habitat is an office. By this point you're healing, no longer leaving a trail of fluids as you move from bedroom to bathroom, no longer wearing a pad in your panties the size of a kitchen sponge to sop it all up. That's also the time human resources will start placing their polite, to-the-point calls about your leave and the date you're expected to return—about your disability benefits and the precise moment they are due to run out. This is also the point where the flowers stop coming and the visitor stream dwindles to a trickle, except for that guy—yes, guy—from the breast pump rental place who brings you the car battery–size contraption and demonstrates how the cold, pinching, wheezing, mechanical thing works, so that you can provide nourishment for your baby from a remote location.

In short, the bubble you've resided in is about to burst as the world beyond nakedly conspires to separate you from your baby. All manner of externals are forming a wedge, and none are more wedgelike than that long line of women who've either been referred to you or answered an ad, who feel fit to step in and take over.

Five minutes before this morning's prospective nanny was due to arrive, I stuffed a sleeping Sophie into her Baby Bjorn, the dark blue front-loading marsupial-type sack you see strapped to the chests of bleary moms and whipped-looking dads everywhere in progressive, baby-heavy neighborhoods like mine on New York's Upper West Side. It was the only position in which Sophie could manage some contentment when not actually nursing, immobilized in the Bjorn against my commodious feed trough of a bosom, her sweaty, crimson scalp just visible above the thickly upholstered infant straitjacket, with its curious nautical motif. In fact, she was so at home in the Bjorn that I frequently carried her around the house like this, wore her broochlike, especially if I was expecting company.

The bell rang; I opened the door. And there stood Hy, almost six feet tall—or so it seemed, given her strong, erect stance (my mind's eye has her filling the doorway). Her black hair was pulled back slick and smart in a meticulously pinned cruller; her dark, appraising, almond-shaped eyes were set deep atop sculpted cheekbones. She wore a matronly skirt and blouse—not her style, I'd come to learn, but surely what she thought a potential employer might approve of.

I managed half a greeting before Hy took over. "You can't carry a baby around like that," she said in a Jamaican accent rich as rum. "She'll never learn to sleep on her own. You have to put her down." And with that she actually began unsnapping the Bjorn and hauling out the sleeping baby inside—*my sleeping baby*—while I dumbly let her. It was the first step, I would come to realize, in the long, fitful process of surrender.

MAKING THE TRANSITION

The trick is in facing the fact that you are going to attempt to construct a starkly bifurcated life, that you will be a mom who also has a career—a secret life, as far as your baby is concerned. Yes, you will happily take on the pain and pleasure of parenthood, but there is a limit to how much you will be available for all the schlepping and pageantry implied. Add to that the almost poignant fact that a good many working women who morph into mothers could safely be described as not quite maternal in the traditional sense, a lot of them being modern, career-track types who never even babysat in their teens; nor did they learn those adjunct skills of conventional momhood: cooking, cleaning, and sewing. Instead, they were busy hitting the books, staying late at their entry-level jobs and putting in long hours at steak houses with their male colleagues— prerequisites of a thriving career in many fields, as is an overweening concentration on *oneself*. (A lawyer friend tells me about her young daughter declaring one day that she wanted to learn how to knit. Momentarily, the mom panicked, having never quite nailed that womanly art. "I was like, God, my grandmother's dead; let me think about this. But then when I tried to teach her, she was like, 'Well, this isn't any fun.' And I said, 'I told you so!'")

"I was not one of those people who felt that there was something missing from my life," a mom who works in publishing tells me, "that I was incomplete; that I'd be completely fulfilled and made whole by the birth of this child. I wanted the baby very much, but I guess what I saw was *the baby*; I didn't necessarily see *me* with the baby." She laughs, and I completely get the humor of it. "I didn't want to be the person dealing with it. Basically, I had to reconcile my new role with the fact that I've always been an independent working person."

She explains: "I always did everything for myself. From a young age, I did my own laundry, did my own typing. People in my family"—sprawling and Irish—"love infants. It makes them feel needed. But for me, I feel the responsibility too greatly. I worry that I might do something wrong, and I have a crazy imagination. It just makes me nervous to have this grave responsibility of a human life." And I applaud this mom's self-knowledge when she says flatly, "I hate being needed"—by everyone but the mover-shaker who employs her, it goes without saying.

The idea that the pleasure of parenthood can be fundamentally abstract, at least in the baby years, is something you hear a lot. Says Jill, whose job it is to manage a record company's Web site, "I am a working person, I instinctively knew that when I gave birth. And I wasn't that happy on maternity leave, just watching CNN while the world was falling apart, the war was about to start, and everybody was looking for Osama Bin Laden. I was like, I can't just sit here nursing and worrying about the world! I didn't handle the idle time well. I knew I had to go back to work."

Although it hardly describes all of them, a good many working mothers of this era are goal-fixated list makers for whom motherhood was less the obvious and evolutionary next step than it was a milestone and a challenge appreciated at first from the neck up, often requiring a bit of a lurch, a graceless tacking off of a well-established course. In talking to working mothers, I'm amused, and a little touched, by the degree to which their once discrete sides so vigilantly maintained start to bleed into each other, the snappy corporate lingo invariably creeping into the realm of the nursery during conversation. For example, one professional woman told me that the notion of a live-in nanny was, for her and her husband, a "nonstarter"; she also spoke of "ratcheting up" her search for a nanny and "vetting" the candidates through and through. Once she hired someone, she told me, it was difficult getting the nanny "into the mix." Maybe it was unconscious, the deeply entrenched parlance of a dyed-in-the-wool corporate creature. But I also got the feeling this was the only way this mother knew to attack a project or task, be it putting together a PowerPoint presentation on projected growth for the fiscal year or finding someone to mind her kid: fast-paced, highly efficient, goal-oriented, with a pinch of dispassion.

Of course, when it goes the other way, when the stuff of the nursery seeps into the corporate realm, things can get a little dicey, given the extent to which self-preserving mothers attempt to downplay the competing demands of family life. Depending on the nature of your workplace, the tolerance for goo-goo ga-ga can be unmercifully low. One New York mom who works for a kid-oblivious single man describes returning to the office after maternity leave to find a sweet surprise from her assistant, who had taken a photograph of the woman's new baby and installed it as the screen saver on her computer. How shocked the woman was to walk into her office and see a TV-sized image of her pink-cheeked dumpling smiling out at her—and anyone else at the firm who happened to walk by. Yes, she was shocked, shocked and horrified. What if her boss swung by and caught a glimpse of this cherubic reminder of her fiercely divided loyalties? In a panic, she instructed her stunned assistant to trash the image immediately and replace it with something generic (one of those cyberish fluorescent dot patterns, no doubt).

My old workplace was full of single, young, childless men. On the rare occasions when my kids visited the office—a wonderland of highlighters, notebooks, paper clips, and spinning chairs on casters—the guys were always nice enough, scouring their offices for anything remotely toylike, a vintage boccie ball, say, or a squirt of shaving cream into the palms of their tiny hands. (It was a men's magazine, so these kinds of manly totems actually were scattered about on any given day.

Not a Playscape nestled in wood chips, but it had its charms.)
And yet I had no illusions about my vulnerability in that free-
balling, testosterone-drenched realm. One night over an
alcohol-fueled work dinner, during a heated exchange between me and a bachelor colleague, he actually riposted with,
"Don't you have some kids to go take care of?"

To be sure, those who attempt this double life are an adven-
turesome, sometimes curious breed. Writing this, I'm reminded of the countless baby showers I've attended for such
women, sitting there on the queen's seat all ironic and gym-
skinny and ropy around the arms and neck, in jarring coun-
terpoint to their brand-new bubble belly that looks strapped
on, opening box after box of baby gear they haven't a clue
how to use—the Diaper Genies, the bottle warmers, the combination baby stroller/infant carrier, the slinglike bouncy seat,
the laughably retro-sounding *layette*. These are the same
women who, in spite of all the love in their hearts, handle
their friends' babies—and in the early days, their own—like a
bag of snakes: arms outstretched, keeping the alien thing at a
safe distance, looking upon it with amusement as it wriggles
and punches and drools its way into their lives.

And yet career women haven't been so denuded of the
good stuff that they don't recognize the life-changing richness
of parenthood. It's not something they want to miss out on,
even if they hadn't fully anticipated the mind-bending logistics. Talk about a challenge: they are doers and achievers, and
they can master this, too.

But it is an artifact of our times that women with lots of options tend to put off getting pregnant, often until they are well into their thirties. And then when they decide it is time to have a kid, they find after decades of assiduous birth control that flipping the switch on the baby-making machinery isn't as easy as it seems. This, too, contributes to a lack of preparedness. Fertility troubles of all kinds are rampant, and the residual drama has complicated the way our generation feels about child care. If years of fruitless fertility treatments lead to the arcane logistics of international adoption, it isn't uncommon for a new mother to sidestep the child-care issue entirely to stay at home full-time with the baby she's moved heaven and earth to get. If she can afford to.

"I'd had so many miscarriages, I couldn't allow myself to even believe I was having a baby," a mother of two tells me. "I had no plan. I didn't have a diaper in the house. Then, about three months after she was born, my mother said, 'Maybe you should get some help.' But I had a lot of fear about this baby that meant the whole world to me. The first time she left the house with somebody else," a twenty-two-year-old sitter, "I thought I was going to die."

Even if the baby came into the world easily, nothing could prepare any of us, so accustomed to plotting our moves, for the pandemonium ahead. "It was really just such a shock," another New York mother tells me about the early days with an infant, after years of office work. "Everything was a slap in the face. The endlessness of it. The day is never over. It's re-

lentless, and no one ever thanks you. Then there's the bitter-
ness and resentment over the fact that only one gender is really
responsible," despite the appearance of a growing parity in the
workplace. "I had no idea how much work a child was. I
guess I spent the whole pregnancy picking out the stroller and
the colors I wanted to decorate the baby's room."

Many of us didn't have a clue what we were getting into, or
what we were going to need along the lines of infrastructure
and support, and our mates were even worse. When I was a
few months pregnant with our first child, my own husband
couldn't understand why we needed to leave the one-bedroom
Greenwich Village apartment we loved, figuring babies are
about as big as a shoebox; how much room, really, would ours
need? At least I'd had some experience with all the plastic gear
and the bodily detritus generated by my nieces when they
were infants years before.

"My husband and I thought we could do it with part-time
help!" says one woman, with a mordant cackle. "We thought
the baby would just lie there and sleep while my husband
writes. I don't know what we were thinking, but we really
envisioned part-time help, and then one of us working while
the baby was sleeping, me going in late to the office. . . . We
thought it would all fall together very neatly, not realizing the
demands and the need for a really structured routine. Of
course, I had a complete breakdown our first night out; my
mother watched our daughter, who was two or three weeks
old. At the restaurant I said, *'No stranger can watch my baby!'* It

was a highly hormonal, highly lactating nightmare. Then about two weeks later, I was like, okay, now we've got to start interviewing people."

FINDING HELP

For many a harassed new mom, day care is a blessed option. At an early age, children get the benefit of sharing and socializing and nailing that iconic life skill: how to play well with others. If the day care's a good one, the people running it are professionals who provide a supportive, instructional environment that's simply more stimulating than the cocoon of home could ever be. Furthermore, as staff, they generally aren't alone: there's at least another colleague or two available to spell them should they start to feel overwhelmed—for many mothers, a real advantage over the solitary nanny scenario. And the cost isn't ruinous—at a few hundred dollars a week, it's less than half what you're likely to pay a full-time nanny.

And yet there are many who cannot stomach the thought of wrenching the tot from his crib every morning and piling him into a taxi or minivan; that, plus making him go momless every day, is simply too much to bear. "I remember my sister who lives in Connecticut telling me about this really cold winter morning when she saw a woman dressed in a suit pulling a really young baby out of the car in the freezing cold and the baby was crying, and she was taking it into a day care in a strip mall," says Debra, a publicist and mother of two. Her eyes widen as her face falls, as though she's telling me about some scandal she's stumbled upon involving infant labor in sweatshops. "It seemed so wrong to me. At that moment I knew I wanted someone to come into our home and be me when I was at work."

Says another mother from a suburb of Boston of the day care she'd sent her first child to, "The revolving door of sullen teenage caregivers, the constant illnesses, packing a bag and sending our baby out every day, it just sucked." So she hired a nanny, which is actually the more economical choice now, given that this mother subsequently had twins and the one nanny takes care of all three. More to the point for women who eschew day care so viscerally, nannies perpetuate the illusion of an around-the-clock mom.

I know that appealed to me. I also liked feeling that the decision to hire help had been forced upon me by the specific limitations of my situation. We made our home in scarifyingly expensive New York City, and my husband, in the fine art field, was in no position to bear the financial burden alone. Of course, all we really had to do to solve our child-care problems was move to a small town, where getting by on one salary isn't a death-defying act. But our dirty little secret was that we had a life in New York that we were unwilling to give up. So once we had decided to stay, I could nurse the notion that my going back to work was a selfless gesture, that the reason I worked was to help pay the bills, when in fact I had a job I had no intention of quitting.

Funny how efficient, motivated, proactive career types are so often relieved when choice is taken away. How many of us in our high-wire midthirties had wished we would just get pregnant "by accident" so as not to have to make that needy-sounding, soul-bearing declaration—if only to ourselves—about *wanting* to have kids. In that sense, the absurd financial demands of New York suited me fine; I was happy to have "no choice" but to pitch in and do my part.

Besides, I suspected I'd make a lousy stay-at-home mother. Although I consider myself to be a very loving mom, I sensed early on how deeply unsuccessful I'd be at the daily minutiae, in the role of camp counselor and cruise director day in and day out. Not only do I feel a crippling lack of the sort of upper-body strength the job demands—hauling strollers, hoisting and shouldering a toddler on the monkey bars, proffering him two-fistedly as he attempts the hand-over-hand, his sneaker-clad feet bouncing off my chin and throat; but I also dreaded the ego abandon required by the endless rounds of peek-a-boo and hide-and-seek, and later, playing cars or Barbies, or any of the other logic and resolution-proof games children crave. For better or worse, having invested so much in my grown-up goals and routines, I suppose I resented the way those games require you to shut off the rest of your life so totally. Kids can smell it when you've got your mind on something else, like the work you left on your desk back at the office, and they won't stand for it. They want all of you, and why shouldn't they? In the early days, you're all they've got.

(The sweetest words ever, which are nonetheless words to kill yourself by as you walk in the apartment after an exhausting day: "Mom," your son says, holding up a handful of brightly colored metal toys, "what car do you want to be?" How about I'll be an opener of mail and a reader of the newspaper? I *so* don't want to be a car.)

I remembered calling my sister, then a stay-at-home mom, on a daily basis when her girls were little. From my end of the phone line it all sounded so chaotic and desperate, so last-chopper-out-of-Saigon—her attempting to entertain and sustain the kids without losing her mind until her husband got home from work. ("Fresh horses" was always how she referred to him, the person at which she thrust the struggling toddlers as he walked in the door.) She told me once about this game they'd play moments before he was due to arrive wherein she'd sit on the floor by the front door, legs outstretched, fashioning them into a canoe shape—a lifeboat, as they appropriately called it—that the kids would jump into. Then they'd all rock together and sing as my sister counted down the seconds until they heard the key slipping into the lock.

Now, I knew I couldn't pull *that* off. It sounded like sheer misery; playing a game like that night after night would kill me. (Do I get points for self-knowledge?) Indeed, I had a sense of my limits. In addition to the temperamental inadequacies, I'm not much of a cook. Or a cleaner, or a shopper. So it would be disastrous for all concerned if I tried to do every bit of it on my own. I felt I had—that phrase again—*no choice* but to hire someone to help me out with some of that heavy lifting at home.

But there was a lot of baggage to sort through first, the specter of my sister's disapproval being only part of it. As a career woman like my mother, I was concerned about replicating some of the less appealing aspects of my upbringing. Of course, when I was growing up in the 1960s, working mothers who raised families in the tightly scripted middle-class exurbs were the exception to the rule, and the lack of any sort of cultural precedent or encouragement or support for what they were trying to accomplish could be devastating. I know it was for my mother, not that she ever complained. In the fun, fizzy early years of our little family in Brooklyn, she actually had help—the sainted Florence, who tended to us expertly Monday through Friday. Although not long after the fateful move to a small, desolate Connecticut town, my mother, all of us, were pretty much on our own.

The Way It Was

My memory of my mother in those days was as a shadowy figure—endlessly dashing around, looking and feeling harassed, slipping out on weekday mornings as my sister and I poured our own bowls of cereal, then racing off in a dilapidated Saab to her job as a school social worker. When she returned, often after five, there was no transitioning, no deft exchanging of one hat for another. Without taking off her coat she would begin tearing open packages of Bird's Eye vegetables, that tasteless boon to the time-challenged mom, and dumping them into pots before settling in with that Holy Grailish thing, a scotch and soda.

That was my father's job—mixing the drinks, after walking the dog and playing a little jazz piano to unwind from his day at work. In that era there was no sense in which a husband wasn't doing his share if he couldn't or wouldn't assist with the meal; men were expected to be delightfully buffoonish in that realm, and it was mold-breaking of him, downright protofeminist, that he actually did the dishes after dinner every night. If my mother had a meeting that kept her out past the dinner hour, it occurred to no one that my father should haul out a casserole dish and produce something edible. Instead he whisked us off to Friendly's for burgers and junior hot fudge sundaes, and it was a treat, a merry all-for-one outing that Mom was never part of.

There was nothing knowingly sexist or negligent about any of this; my father was simply doing what men did in those days. Of course, by the status-quo-flouting seventies, he was quick to make the appropriate adjustments, actually perfecting a dish of his own to serve on my mother's increasingly frequent late nights out, something involving chicken and fat slices of oranges and onions that derived from an old Jewish recipe. Chicken à la Walter, he called it, after himself, which he would unveil with an oven-mitted flourish that made us laugh. To us it was pure charm and fatherly selflessness, this occasional meal, something to applaud and enjoy. In those days, fathers got so much praise for their intermittent little stabs at domesticity and nurture; with glamorous-sounding one-offs like the school-sponsored "father-daughter night," it took very little to meet the basic requirements. Indeed, there was no percentage in going overboard, lest they be looked upon as unmanly.

Although it shames me to say it now, while we thoroughly appreciated Chicken à la Walter, we greeted every morsel of my mother's hastily prepared repasts with nothing but sullen contempt. And no, the food wasn't really something to celebrate; I think I could taste the hostility, her corrosive ambivalence toward this part of the job. She had no time for it and not a lot of interest; the attentiveness required did not sit right with a woman so wrapped up in her own emotionally demanding work. But she had no choice. This was her role and she did her best, despite being out of step with most of the other mothers in the community, the local crust trimmers and snack providers and juice pourers who gave the impression of being virtually on hold until their children returned from school.

At least that's how I saw them during time spent at friends' homes. For me it is an image of incalculable, enduring significance: the matched set of three graham crackers on colorful plastic plates, Kool-Aid in cups, and white paper napkins folded into large triangles all laid out for me and my friend

Kate by her efficient, smiling mom when we'd go to her tidy house after school. At my house? A high-strung German shepherd that minded the place until my parents came home from work two hours later.

It would take years, decades, for me to understand why my mother struggled so, why it was often so flustering and isolating to be her; it would take easily as long to realize how heroic she was for pursuing her passions in that difficult era, and what a fine, if fraught, example she set. (I wound up pretty much emulating her, didn't I?) At the time, all I could do was covet what I lacked, an upbeat servant making tasty treats in the kitchen, all for the joy of seeing me happy.

Now I realize all I really wanted was that lowly, prosaic thing all kids crave at a certain point: to be normal, to have what everyone else had. I think it's why I developed a fetish for sandwiches, of all things, and what they represented, the sort of mom-based middle-American brand of nurture depicted so relentlessly in TV commercials: bland, white-bread, packaged, bought-in-bulk, the cornerstone of that mommade thing, the bag lunch. Oh, how I wanted a piece of that dull dream. One day when several friends had come over to my house to work on a school project (my mother as usual being out, doing one thing or another), I attempted to suggest the presence of an attentive, bustling provider stashed in the back somewhere by making a platter full of peanut-butter-and-Fluff sandwiches beforehand, carefully cut and jauntily stacked; it was a baldly subversive choice, given my mother's disdain for low-end crap like Fluff. Then I covered them carefully with a sheet of foil and crimped the edges around the perimeter of the plate, the way TV moms do. What I didn't realize until it was too late was that the sandwich crowd had pretty much moved off PB-and-Fluff by that point—on to what, I had no way of knowing. And so, when I ceremoniously brought out the platter and removed the foil, the girls sniffed. That day the sandwiches pretty much went untouched.

Of course, so much in childhood isn't what it seemed; turns out brown-bagging it is a bore, the overripe in-crowd prematurely goes to seed, and not a few snack-packing moms, more conflicted deep down than we could ever have known, turn to drink, get divorced, move, meditate, get a job, having fought their way out of a stultifying role that's a hell of a lot harder to play than it looks. The furthest thing from the source of homespun satisfaction we might have imagined.

By the time I was figuring out how I'd be raising my own kids, the mother's lot had blessedly changed; there simply were more acceptable ways to be one. I certainly was never made to feel like a foolhardy frontierswoman, a crazy loner, for pursuing a career. And you can bet I landed a man who's good with a recipe and a sharp kitchen knife. Who easily, and for the most part cheerfully, does a full 90 percent of the grocery shopping for the family.

But I knew the potential still existed for raising kids who resented their mother for having other interests—obligations and commitments that took her away from them. The culture may have expanded its idea of what a mother can be, but babies—those wrinkly, altogether unenlightened taskmasters—have not. They are still tickled and cheered in a uniquely primal way by the big smiling face they see most often, by the person who comes running when they cry.

So here was the challenge: I needed to find someone who would take impeccable care of my new daughter. But I needed to feel really good about it, too—as guilt free and unconflicted as possible. I couldn't suffer in silence; I couldn't let my child see the strain. And when one expert or another would opine in print about the developmental benefits of a child's being able to form attachments with an adult *outside* the parental unit, I clung to the findings like smeared banana to a baby's face. Something about trust, perspective, emotional equilibrium—whatever. Nothing, with the possible exception of the news that a glass of wine is actually good for your heart, could have cheered me more.

AND NANNY MAKES FOUR

Y OU MAKE THE decision to hire someone, to do your
level best to create some maternal facsimile at home.
Now comes the hard part: whom will you hire? No, it's not
like choosing an assistant or a contractor or a tax guy. It's
slightly dumbfounding, what you're asking this theoretical
employee to do, and finding her is a lot harder than you ever
pictured.

One of the most unnerving aspects of a mother's relationship with a nanny is the often haphazard, ill-conceived way it
comes to be. How strange that women with advanced degrees and vast research projects to their credit can go about
such an important decision so blindly, often jotting down
names from hand-scrawled ads, tearing off phone numbers
from bulletin boards and telephone poles beside ads for Pilates classes and used bikes. I know a woman of awe-inspiring
corporate skill, the smoking BlackBerry sort who can access
a number for any maitre d' of consequence in a matter of

moments, who nonetheless hired a nanny without managing to get her last name, let alone her husband's name or what borough of New York they live in. It might sound unthinkable, but in fact it's not: by no means does workplace efficiency translate to this unregulated, denial-rife realm. As for me, "research" amounted to my haunting the parks—first as an extremely pregnant person, then with my infant—trying to assess what constituted a good nanny pretty much by watching them. In other words, a whole hell of a lot was riding on my gut.

"The single most eye-opening experience ever was spending all day in the park with all the nannies," Sharon, a mother of two, relatively new to New York, tells me. "Where we'd been living in Chicago was suburban, so I'd never seen the variety of nanny and parenting styles that you see in a New York park. And at the time it was just disturbing, shocking, and rewarding, refreshing, all the adjectives you could think of. There were the bench nannies, the ones who sit over there and allow their kids to run wild and urinate freely on one another," she says with a smirk. "There were the nannies who are really caring and loving, and the ones who are borderline abusive. And you just sit there and think, *How can you make this decision?* How do you know you're hiring the one who is *that* nanny and not that one over there? I'm sure they all seem like the right kind face-to-face. It's just so troubling to think that something could happen, and the children can't speak for themselves."

NANNY SHOPPING

In my interviews with mothers, there is a question I asked them all: when you went about hiring a nanny, what qualities were you looking for? Obvious enough. Although in the case of working women, I was fairly certain that most weren't necessarily looking for clones of themselves. For many of them, the whole point is that they were farming out a part of this job that they, for whatever reason, weren't able to perform, and the idea that they had to supplement themselves in some way and compensate for the areas in which they were lacking struck me as being potentially loaded.

Most mothers admit that it all seemed pretty straightforward at first. "I thought I wanted someone like me," says Marlene, who works in the fashion industry. "Someone who could multitask, because I have so much energy. But what I realized after interviewing people was that I just wanted someone who was going to love the baby. Before they're born, you have an idea of what you want in a nanny, but you don't really know the job yet. You don't have the baby in your arms, and you don't know how protective you'll feel about this child."

So you start out with the obvious one: love, love, and more love should do the trick. "I just knew it was important to find someone who loved my child and who was responsible and who was going to hold and hug and kiss and love and watch her and be safe and have the right training," Jill, the Web site manager tells me. "Do they know CPR? Have they taken care of children before? What have they done in an emergency situation? I also wanted someone who was bright. It wasn't a question of whether their English was perfect; it was whether or not they had an alertness and a sense of urgency. Will you not take your eyes off my child at the playground? Will you call me immediately? Will you keep your cell phone on? You're taking care of someone else's flesh and blood; it is *not* a regular job."

But aside from the CPR, how can you divine any of that in a thirty-minute chat? First impressions can be very misleading. As you stare into the pleasant, unreadable face of one stranger after another, you find yourself wondering, *Are you my baby's nanny?* The nettlesome vagueness, the unquantifiableness of it all. As one woman poignantly put it to me, "More than anything, I was looking for someone who was *warm*"—although another adds an intriguing twist: "I never wanted her to be like a mother, because *I* was the mother."

Bulletin: Virtually all moms are in agreement that sweet, loving, competent women tend to make the best nannies. However, move past those criteria and there's a whole host of loopy, seemingly arbitrary considerations a new mother can't begin to anticipate until she is in the thick of the hiring process.

For example, you are certainly not the sort of person to hold it against someone if she is a little bit overweight. But do you want someone lugging around extra pounds if her job is to chase after your toddler and get to him before he wanders into harm's way? Suddenly physique, of all things, threatens to become an issue (the stuff of lawsuits, in other professions). Surely how someone dresses isn't a meaningful reflection of how she would care for a child. But why do you find yourself gravitating toward candidates whose sense of style you appreciate? Is *taste* in any way relevant to the job? The nanny will frequently be dressing your children, after all. Given the deeply personal nature of the job, it isn't unreasonable to think that the way a candidate puts herself together could, for some women, be a deal breaker.

"We had this one college student show up," says Mary, a mother of two boys in Manhattan. "I guess I should have gotten a heads up from her e-mail address, which was something like meeesooohot@hotmail.com. But I was like, well, college kids, they have their wacky ways, so all right, fine. And she was very, very sweet on the phone. She said she grew up in the Bronx and had five brothers and sisters and a lot of cousins and had done a lot of babysitting.

"So she rang the bell and my husband opened the door. And then he came back to where I was and said, 'Did you get me a hooker for my birthday?'

"Spiky silver high heels, white fishnet stockings—not panty hose, but thigh-high stockings. A micromini white ruffled skirt; midriff shirt, low-cut, big boobs spilling out; tons of makeup; silver lipstick. Her hair was all up in this ponytail with little tendrils coming down. She was *exuding* scent. So I give her a cursory little interview before shoving her the hell out of my life, because I'm just, like, what drugs do you think I'm on that I'm gonna hire you?"

Given the stakes—the unreal level of faith and trust you're preparing to put into this stranger—a fair amount of hair splitting, labeling, and judgment rendering can be expected. Yes, it is any woman's prerogative to accessorize herself as she likes, wearing, say, lacquered, gem-studded synthetic nails two inches long. But are those really the loving hands you picture wrapped around your baby? No, you are not an ageist; how lovely and grandmotherly the nanny who's an old pro, graying at the temples and comfortably set in her ways. But can she keep up with your kid? Does she have those deep reservoirs of energy for constant entertainment that you yourself most certainly do not?

Yes, you'll expect to have some sort of emotional attachment to whomever you hire; you'll hope she is happy and has a rich and satisfying life beyond the job. But why are you unnerved by the idea of your nanny having boyfriends, ex-husbands, and teenage kids? Why are you hoping for someone a tad . . . *hermetic*?

Several women I talked to include on the list of their nannies' virtues a devotedness to the job only made possible by a near absence of anything else in their worlds. "She doesn't have much of a life," one mother tells me about the live-in woman she hired. "She came to this country to make money. She has a cousin and a brother in Queens. That's it. She's never called in sick, ever, not once. She takes vacation when we take vacation. If she ever wanted to go do something, she could ask me or tell me, but she doesn't. She'd rather be in the house." Does she get phone calls? "Never. Not one." It's but one of the factors that have made her a very attractive nanny.

Some mothers look for shared values. Jean from suburban Boston advertised for a nanny on her church bulletin board, hoping for a God-fearer. "I am a sometimes, heh, practicing Catholic," she says, "and while it wasn't essential to me that our new nanny also be a member of the Catholic faith, I thought it would be good to get someone who, you know, believes in God at least. Not that that guarantees your child's safety or anything, but in some way this was me putting it in God's hands." Yet even those women who've sworn off anything resembling organized religion in their own lives tend to swoon over the widow nannies who live alone, carry a well-worn Bible, and devote their weekends to church.

Who wouldn't? Aspiring to that in a nanny, indulging that fantasy, isn't so unreasonable. What is unreasonable are the hours some women expect the employee of their dreams to work; their even thinking a regular twelve-hour shift is viable is a measure of their inexperience. "I do not regard myself as a counselor, even though I have a counseling background," says Denise Landry, who runs a nanny agency in New York City. "And if the mothers aren't asking my advice, it's not my place to give it. But if I see something that's patently going to be contrary to what is possible, I have the right to say, 'Look,

7:30 to 7:30 is a very difficult schedule. I'm not judging you, but do you think you could possibly adjust it?'"

Not only is that a punishing shift, but what of the mother who, with coverage like that, is probably never going to see her kid? "I cannot conceive of being away from a young child twelve hours a day," says Landry. "Some nannies I've spoken with say the parents"—even the kind, loving ones—"just don't understand the sacrifices that come with being a parent."

There are those, for instance, who are so overwhelmed that the only solution they can rightly imagine is live-in round-the-clock help. A perfectly okay option if the situation can support it; a delusional plan if it can't. "I'll say, 'Do you have accommodations?'" says Landry, of those who come looking for a live-in nanny. "They say, 'Well, she can sleep with the baby.' And again I'll say, 'I'm not judging you, but you want somebody who at the end of the day can talk to a friend and watch a television program, and you're nanny's not going to be able to do this.' It's that indentured servant mentality." Which hints at the ticklish subject of race.

It's the creeping subtext of so many mother-nanny relation-ships, the glaring difference between you—the factor that dare not speak its name. And yet, get out on the mom circuit and you will be stunned by the openness with which it's discussed—the clinical specificity with which women parse the relative merits of one ethnic variety of nanny over another. In conversation, nationalities are tossed around as casually as paint colors and ice cream flavors. Indeed, there is a risible whiff of *shopping* to all of this, of comparing labels, from down-market to designer. One woman I know is so proud of having landed a flaxen-haired nanny that she drops regular anecdotes about the girl's amusing, home-spun Swedishness, code in the nanny realm—or in any realm, I suppose—for *white.* (Of course, white nannies tend to draw a higher salary, so for some people there is an element of status in being able to afford one. It's something to be crowed about, like granite countertops.)

"Most nannies here are Mexican and Central American," says L.A.-based playwright Lisa Loomer, whose play *Living Out* concerns a Latina's efforts to do right by her child by taking care of someone else's (a wealthy white family's in Southern California). "And I've encountered really crazy prejudices and preconceptions about Latina nannies. Everything from 'They're hardworking' to 'They lie.' Some people don't want too young, some people don't want too sexy. There's definitely a hierarchy about skin color, weight, age. A lot of people favor lighter-skinned, slimmer nannies, and yet some don't want them to be *too* slim and *too* pretty, because they're concerned about their husbands. Some worry about imperfect English and their children learning it from them."

There are perfectly good reasons for hiring a nanny from one part of the world or another, perhaps the best having to do with the language they speak. A Chinese American friend of mine has always had Chinese help for her three kids for the simple reason that she wants them to be bilingual and exposed to that part of their heritage. More often than not, though, decisions are informed by the gross assumptions that are made about the quality and character of one race over another.

A friend of a friend actually recommends that mothers "go Filipino," so enamored was she of her nanny's servile efficiency, which she took to be an ethnic trait. "Women from the Caribbean," she says, "I'd never do that again. Never." With the Filipina nanny, "there was no attitude, no laziness, and she was smart. There isn't a beat that this woman misses."

Says another fan of the Philippines, "I hate to make these generalizations, but Filipinos are much more formal than Jamaicans, probably, or Latinos, or whatever. They're definitely not as friendly, more standoffish. But I do think Filipinos are more detail-oriented. You can tell them something and they do it exactly the way you tell them, which I love. Like, 'make the bed this way,' and they'll do it that way. I also think Filipinos are more even-keeled, which, in the beginning, is good. They don't get thrown by the child crying all the time." (More palatably, one mother swears by nannies from the West Indies, which she calls "a nice culture. They make fried plantains, and my kids love fried plantains.")

Perhaps it's no surprise that the darker the skin, the more thoughtlessly damning the stereotypes. One day while very pregnant, I ran into a well-heeled male friend on the street who had a couple of kids in elementary school. He was curious about my plans for going back to work and finding care for the new baby. Then he stated it decisively: "Avoid women from the Islands"—the Trinidadians, the Grenadans, the Jamaicans—"because they're really bossy." Oh, I said, okay. Thanks for the heads-up.

That evening when I reported this fascinating insight to my husband, that we should "avoid women from the Islands," he, to his everlasting credit, was appalled. That bit of advice was straight-up ignorant, if not racist, as far as he was concerned, and I felt ashamed for having tolerated it, even for one hormone-addled moment.

That said, for the well-intentioned, it's easy to overthink things. According to one Manhattan mother of two, "I had a knee-jerk response to the fact that everybody's babysitter I saw was African American, or Caribbean American, taking care of white children, and I didn't think that's what I wanted to do." That is, she didn't want to participate in a system so stereotype-driven, so racially prescribed. So racist. "But then I thought, well, that's reverse prejudice"—denying a woman a job because of the color of her skin. She wound up hiring a wonderful woman from Trinidad.

As it happened, all the women I interviewed—maybe five—were from "the Islands." And yes, I too was on the hunt for warmth. The sort of nanny I knew I did *not* want was one who had left small children in her home country in order to come to the States to make money. I couldn't imagine asking someone to love *my* kids when that job had required her to abandon (at least physically) her own. It seemed almost immoral, just too much to ask.

During a conversation with one prospective nanny from the Caribbean about what I was looking for, I had the opportunity to share this bit of virtuousness. Fully expecting the candidate to applaud my sensitivity, I was surprised when instead she fixed me with a long, hard, what-is-it-with-you-white-women stare. Finally she said, "But those women really need the job. They need to send money home to their kids." Slowly it dawned on me what deep waters I was wading into.

An envoy of the complacent, choice-laden land of plenty parsing ethics with someone who knows the real meaning of desperation—culturally speaking, it's where the rubber meets the road. A few years ago at a gathering, I met the former student of a high school teacher friend, a beautiful self-made Seven Sisters graduate whose parents grew up in Jamaica. Thinking I'd found suitable common ground for small talk, I mentioned our fond association with Jamaica, given that our kids' nanny is from there. As I blithely spoke about Hy's hometown and our hopes of visiting someday, the young woman visibly stiffened, her eyes narrowing. And I give her credit for coming out with it. After a short but scrupulously maintained silence, she basically said that she's sick of *nannies* being the subject that always comes up when dealing with people like, well, me; although she didn't put it quite this way, she wanted me to know that the Caribbean is more than an exploitable-domestic-worker factory.

She went on to talk about her boyfriend's mother, and how much she disapproved of her subjecting herself to that humiliating job. At which point I had to object, feeling protective of this woman I'd never even met—as well as of Hy and our wholehearted deal. I also felt more knowing than she was about what her boyfriend's mother had most likely been up against. Generationally speaking, I was certain the mother had faced far fewer options than my new friend here. She'd bravely done the best she could, under the circumstances. And I said as much.

But the former student wouldn't have any of it. She had made it on her own, she said, having slipped the socioeconomic stranglehold, defying the expectations of my kind; why can't everyone else?

I thought her rhetorical impetuousness was way off, but her personal stake, and the unexpected force of her anger, put me to my knees. Without question she won the round.

One of my greatest concerns about hiring a woman of color was the idea of perpetuating that highly visible and somewhat eerie cultural dynamic that finds blacks caring for whites at the most vulnerable periods in our lives—when we're babies and geriatrics; them pushing us around on sunny days in the park in one wheeled conveyance or another, feeding us soft food and wiping the dribble from our chins, keeping us company, jollying us in saccharine falsettos. You see this played out around preschools and retirement homes far and wide: the infinitely patient black woman helping the compromised Caucasian, be he newborn or elderly, to get through the day.

But what of the white person's empire-building middle years, all fifty of them? Where are the black people then? Generally speaking, there are few respectable places made for them in the better part of a white person's life.

If we were to wind up hiring a dark-skinned person with an exotic accent, as so many parents in the neighborhood had done, I didn't want my children thinking these women had been placed on earth expressly for this purpose, for their safe-keeping, their pleasure. Despite its looking as though every baby automatically was assigned one of his own at birth, I needed the kids to know that a Caribbean nanny isn't some sort of fabulous accessory—something that just comes with the teething ring and the monogrammed cup: a smiling, knowing, fanciful life-chaperone who had been beamed here from some storied land, and who would one day disappear as magically as she'd come. If we were to hire a woman from "the Islands," I vowed to drive the point home to my kids that she had a rich and complicated life of her own that began long before either of them were born, and was sure to con-tinue well beyond her time with us.

THE INTERVIEW

Many of the mothers in the new nanny class don't come from wealthy stock; they're wage slaves who've always worked and have never known anything else. They aren't necessarily accustomed to hiring people, or to being bosses, particularly in their own homes.

"When I was growing up, nannies weren't even in the realm of my social sphere," says Lina, a working mother in the Washington, D.C., area who has a two-year-old son. "And I was very uncomfortable at first being a boss and figuring out what my relationship with Jocelyn [her Trinidadian nanny] was. In the beginning, I was kind of embarrassed to hand her the check at the end of the week. It was like, who do I think I am to have a nanny?"

If the role is, at bottom, hopelessly alien, the mother can count on committing blunders, particularly at the beginning. It's what makes the interview process such an awkward one. So often the woman doing the hiring doesn't really know what questions to ask, what, exactly, she's supposed to be looking for; nor does she feel entitled to pose questions in the first place.

In the best of worlds, she's businesslike about it: where are you from, what's your level of experience, how have you coped in emergency situations, and so on. But a lot of mothers new to the role have a hard time being that direct. They want so badly to come across as decent and postcolonial, trusting and unintrusive, that they neglect to ask important questions like whether the woman can drive, can swim, can read well, given the medicine labels and street signs she'll surely be encountering with tot in tow in the normal course of the job. But who wants to ask that? Although it's completely unconscious, sometimes it seems mothers would rather suffer the consequences of not knowing than put the difficult questions and concerns on the table.

"I really wanted someone who could read to my kids, and I didn't know how to ask that without sounding . . . It's kind of racist to suggest that somebody [from a third-world country] isn't a good reader," Janine says. "But I would just feel so inappropriate asking that question, so I wasn't able to do it. And my nanny's a bad reader. She's not even a very good speaker"—by American standards. In fact, stumped by her thick Guyanese accent during the interview, Janine asked her what her first language was. "English!" the nanny replied, somewhat indignantly.

I think a lot of us are just so overwhelmed by the newness of it all, so ambivalent about the chapter unfolding, that we check our good sense at the rattan welcome mat. Yes, you'll do your best to make a good decision, contacting every applicant's references, although as one mother puts it, "I think references are the biggest pile of bullshit in the world. Because everyone's living in their own Pollyanna world." Meaning, they are invested to a delusional degree in their own nanny's mythical perfection. "References are preposterous, except maybe if the nanny's been with the family a hundred years."

An overwhelming need for it all to work out and be good has a way of undermining a mom. As one otherwise high-functioning mother put it to me, "I didn't know *what* I was doing."

Assuming you've chosen to punt on the reading question, the most awkward—and most indispensable—part of the in-home interview comes when the candidate is expected to gather up and cuddle the baby by way of demonstrating her magical facility with kids. It's like some dreadful mating ritual in which animals are thrown together for potential breeding; interested parties gather round and watch, wondering if they're going to take to one another. Mothers aren't thrilled to be handing over their infants, and everyone's mortified if the baby erupts in red-faced screams once she does. In the best-case scenario the nanny holds the swaddled bundle close and smiles and clucks her tongue and coos, transfixing the baby, a look of wishnik delight spreading across his crinkly face. She's a master at this and she knows it, the nanny's serene, broad smile seems to say. But the tricky truth of the role is revealed: this woman has just met you both and cares nothing for either of you, yet she can turn on the love and the fun in an instant, as needed. Yes, even stranger-babies can be fun to hold, but in this scenario she's doing a job. This is a skill she possesses, not, for the most part, an emotion she's expressing. And that is something you'll have to get used to.

During the interview, the candidate will say all the right things; for instance, that she loves kids but disapproves of TV and junk food and Game Boys. But who *is* this woman, really? How can you find out what it is she's made of?

"*What to Expect When You're Expecting* has this great list of questions to ask a nanny," Debra, the publicist, says, "and one of them was, What's her favorite book to read to her children and the children she babysat for? That question was key for me. So I asked Ginger that, and she said, 'Dr. Seuss,' and I *love* Dr. Seuss, the morals and the fun. And I think you need a certain kind of personality to get it."

Well sure, why not? Still and all, this is an awfully slender piece of information when trying to determine a person's fitness for what, from your perspective, is the most important job in the world. Nonetheless, says Debra of her interview with Ginger, "She came through with flying colors."

Indeed, sometimes the most trivial attributes make the difference in this crucial decision. For one mother, finding a nanny who wouldn't complain about the fact that they live in a fifth-floor walk-up was the key. "When most of them came upstairs, they'd be huffing and puffing," she says. "But Gayle didn't care. She took her shoes off and came in." And yes, she got the job.

In my case, I'd ask these wildly open-ended questions like, "How do you deal with it if you're feeling angry with a child?" After a couple of nerve-shredding weeks in the new role of mother, I saw how easily things could get out of hand. I worried about any of these women being as close to the breaking point as I seemed to be a dozen times a day. And yet they'd smile and dismiss it as a nonissue—they love children! How could anyone get angry at a little baby? There was no reasonable way of assessing these vague, well-meaning responses. Posing theoretical questions like this seemed an entirely seat-of-the-pants way of attempting to make a hire.

Difficult—borderline absurd—as it is, mothers have to make judgments in the little time they're given, sometimes on the basis of scant conversation. "Jen came with her brother for the interview; he did most of the talking," says Diane, who was looking for a sitter for her infant son. "She had come straight from Trinidad. The thing that made me know she was right was that she came from a big family, and that was important to her. I trusted her that way. I didn't know a thing about babies two months before, and she wasn't really a nanny. But she had her own daughter, she loved kids, has tons of nieces and nephews, and she wanted to work. That's what I cared about." Besides—and we know how appealing this can be— she was alone. She could give everything to the job. "I didn't want some weird boyfriend hanging out in my house."

When the time came for me to interview candidates for the job of minding my own kid, like most mothers, I was going on instinct. One woman arrived late because her child was sick, and I knew that situation wouldn't work out over the long haul; at that moment I pretty much crossed women with small children of their own off the list—not pausing to contemplate my desire for someone who essentially wasn't needed by anyone but us.

Another woman came accompanied by a friend who sat in the corner throughout our interview; not the worst thing in the world, I suppose, although I found myself agitated by the implication that she felt she might need some sort of protection from me.

Yet another seemed incredibly sweet but . . . well, the silliest things can put you off: she had a way of touching her face incessantly as we talked, sort of running her fingertip along the corners of her mouth; she also had a stuffy nose, and I guess I hoped for someone a bit more anal about germs. These are the horrible little assessments and snap judgments you find yourself making about someone who might be the world's best and most responsible person, but then you'll never get to experience that, will you?

As if the Dadaist interrogation technique weren't painful enough for all concerned, when a candidate has the luck of advancing to the next level, what that means is she'll be asked to venture outside the home, down the street and perhaps to the playground, to demonstrate her strolling skills, her handling of traffic—accompanied by the first-time mom, of course. On these nakedly obvious, arranged "first dates," these comically stilted outings, the mothers tend to be higher maintenance than the babies. I've witnessed them on several occasions: the white mother fidgety and fluttering alongside a carriage that is being pushed by the expressionless third-world nanny candidate—the strained interaction is almost unbearable to witness.

"One time when I was trying out this woman from Mexico, I went into a store and I left her with my daughter, and when I came out they were nowhere. I'm like, Oh my God, *she's stolen my baby!*" Marlene tells me with a rueful laugh. "And all she'd done was walk down the street, but I was totally freaked out."

That said, this frantic exercise with the women she interviewed actually proved to be clarifying. With Eva, the nanny she finally hired, Marlene had been impressed that "Once they reached the corner, she would always stand back in the shade and wait for the traffic and noise to pass, while others would push the stroller right up to the corner. I thought, Eva's someone who thinks about those things." It was the trait that tipped the balance—notwithstanding the fact that shortly after Eva came aboard, Marlene had another panic attack when she and the baby were a half hour late (having mistaken "quarter of" for "quarter after"); Marlene was on her way to fetch the cops when Eva calmly emerged from the playground, precious young'un in tow. Blessed with the perspective that comes with experience, Marlene now knows what a hopeless neophyte she was at the time; kudos to Eva for being able to endure it.

A pleasing manner, energy, good taste in kids' books, *warmth*—these are but some of the traits mothers want to see in the women they hire. In our overanalyzed, middle-class lives, we have the luxury to require such things, and cut the distinctions that finely if we so choose, if we're able. What is rarely considered in these decorous interviews is the grim necessity that often drives immigrant women to answer an ad for a job like this. If there is tension between employer and employee, some of it takes root here, in the vastly different circumstances that have brought them together.

THE GREAT DIVIDE

Your mutual need—for help, for a job—and your shared stake in the rearing of kids is why you are sitting across from each other now. Beyond that, you're in utterly different places, having been dealt very different cards.

One isn't likely to learn the extreme backstories in an interview, but they are there. Brenda had been working as a bus conductor in Barbados when in 1993 Barbados needed to apply to the World Bank for a loan. To qualify for it, the country had to devalue its currency, resulting in something called a "structural adjustment," an antiseptic name for a devastating process in which a wide swath of public services and jobs are reduced, cut, or phased out, which is how Brenda lost her job. The bus conductors were replaced by fare boxes. Nearly a thousand people were suddenly out of work. Brenda interviewed at the unemployment office, but they had nothing for her.

What made the situation especially grim was that Brenda had recently arranged for some home improvements and was saddled with loans, as well as four children. Her husband couldn't support the family on his bus driver salary, so she had to find work. A sister was already in America taking care of children, and Brenda decided to follow suit.

"The hardest thing was that my oldest son had a baby from a young girl, and I was taking care of it," Brenda says. "Many nights I just cried because I had to leave him. It was really,

really hard. I don't remember anything in my life that was harder than that, to leave William." She wipes her eyes. "He's sixteen now."

The contexts, the circumstances are unthinkable. I hear about another woman, a widow with six children who had been a nanny for the family of a Belgian diplomat in the Congo, who was relocating to the United States. In order to support her own children, she had to keep her job with the diplomat and leave the kids behind. Loneliness, missing them, was the least of her problems, as she was expected to work around the clock with no overtime pay or days off for someone who should have known better, someone who treated her like property; alone and far from home, she simply was that much easier to exploit.

Ginger from Guyana also found herself unable to provide for her three children after her husband died of a heart attack when she was only thirty-seven. Theoretically, she could have forced her eldest son to drop out of school and help out, but Ginger was unwilling to do that. Instead, she left behind everything she knew and tried her luck in the States so that she could provide from afar. Despite the agreeable climate of Florida, where she had a sister, she didn't drive and was uncomfortable in a car culture. A move to New York City was inevitable.

"I don't have any kids," says May, who is in her fifties and wears her hair short, in tight curls. She's on the couch at her employer's place on the Upper West Side with a cat on her lap, her bare feet crossed at the ankles. "I was pregnant about three times, but I can't really carry them full-term. I would have to be lying on my back for the next nine months, so it didn't work out.

"I had a bad relationship with a boyfriend in Barbados. He got very abusive," she says. "I could go nowhere without him knowing where I was going. We had this festival at the end of sugar cane season, this carnival kind of thing, and I went to that. And when I came back, I couldn't get into the house; he had completely changed the locks. It was a shame, because the festival was a real beautiful thing.

"The yelling part I could probably live with, but it was the words that came after . . . I'd just had enough. A friend of mine was living here and she said, 'You don't have to stay there; whenever you're ready, just let me know.' I had my visa already, so all I did was buy my ticket and call her and tell her, and she said fine."

Once in New York, the culture shock was greater than May could have imagined. "You don't have buildings like this in Barbados; everything is flat, like in Florida," she says. "And one day I saw this animal running on the wire, and I said to my friend, 'What is a mongoose doin' up on the wire?' And she said, 'It's not a mongoose, it's a squirrel!'" May laughs. "I used to stare out the window watching these animals running from tree to tree.

"And the snow! I remember the first time I saw it. I just lied on my bed in the Bronx, watching it coming down, and writing letters to everyone back home, and telling them about the snow." Describing this, May wears an expression that's grown familiar to me from my interviews with nannies: relief, coupled with wistfulness. So many have come so far, in every sense. But they've paid a price. For most of them, a profound sense of loneliness and homesickness is simply part of the job.

If you're supported, privileged, fat with choice, an immigrant's straits are hard to comprehend. Celia, who is twenty-five and from Colombia, came to New York City five years ago. The idea was to join her mother, who'd been driven here years before by financial desperation—one factor, surely, in the breakup of her marriage to Celia's father. (When women immigrate here for jobs in domestic labor, marriages are common casualties.)

"She used to have a business back in my country, a stationery and book store for ten or twelve years," Celia says. "But then the economy went really bad. She didn't know anybody when she came. She had to sleep in the subway station sometimes."

As lousy as that sounded, Celia saw no future for herself in Colombia and so decided to join her mother in New York. "If you're a girl there, you're supposed to get married," she says. "If you're lucky, you can afford to go to university, but my parents couldn't afford it." Besides, she wasn't getting along with her father, and she missed her mother terribly. So here she is, a second-generation nanny in New York.

Survival in some cases, the need to make a wage and provide

for kids, the dream of a better life, facing the sort of odds most of us will never know, craving the very rudiments of well-being that all of us take for granted . . . these are the kinds of situations that propel a woman from the third world thousands of miles from her home into ours.

The unprecedented influx of women from economically unstable places like the Caribbean, the Philippines, and Central America came on the heels of a period of so-called enlightenment in this country, when American black women spurred by civil rights and feminism began saying no to domestic work, to the child-care and cleaning jobs that had historically been their fate. Sensitive, educated white women had no choice but to throw their support behind them. Who, then, was going to mind the house and kids? Help, as it happened, was on the way. In *Atlantic* magazine in March of 2004, post-feminist valkyrie Caitlin Flanagan described it memorably:

> [L]ike magic, as though the fairy god-mother of women's liberation had waved a starry wand, the whole problem got solved. You must take a deus ex machina where you find one, and in the case of the crumbs and jelly on the counter tops, the deus ex machina turned out to be the forces of global capitalism. With the arrival of a cheap, easily exploited army of poor and luckless women, fleeing famine, war, the worst kind of poverty, leaving behind their children to do it, facing the possibility of rape or death on the expensive and secret journey, one

of the noblest tenets of second-wave feminism collapsed like a house of cards. The new immigrants were met at the docks not by a highly organized and politically powerful group of American women intent on bettering the lot of their sex but, rather, by an equally large army of educated professional-class women with booming careers who needed their children looked after and their house cleaned. Any supposed equivocations about the moral justness of white women's employing dark-skinned women to do their shit work simply evaporated.

Flanagan's patented hyperbole can be risible; for starters, a lot of the duties these women are asked to perform aren't "shit work"—not even remotely. In significant part, it's the tender bits, the companionship, the snuggles and hugs that they are paid to supply daily, which any mother outsources with a heavy heart. But Flanagan's larger point is as irrefutable as it is tough to swallow: wittingly or not, we are the beneficiaries of these women's desperation.

Mothers analyze that fact reluctantly and scan the abundant literature at their peril. Along with books like *When Mothers Work*—whose sober title sounds like a cooked-up pathology, something akin to loving too much—the specter of Barbara Ehrenreich and Arlie Russell Hochschild looms. Hochschild wrote (and Ehrenreich ecstatically blurbed) *The Commercialization of Intimate Life,* which illustrates, among other things, how we have become consumerist gluttons for coddling and care, using all that filthy, frantically earned lucre to hire nurturers and helpers, as opposed to providing any of that ourselves.

Of course she has a good point: from the booking of venues and planners and entertainers for kids' birthday parties to the rampant use of tutors, the overscheduled middle and upper classes often seem more at home writing a check than taking a crack at the increasingly ancient art of parenting itself. Who could have imagined a few decades ago that there'd one day be a thriving industry of faux parents, whom you can hire to teach your kids how to bake, throw a baseball, and ride a bike?

Global Women—an anthology that examines the causes and consequences of third-world women migrating to the United States for a life-saving wage, coedited by Ehrenreich and Hochschild—forces readers to ask themselves if their bourgeois needs perpetuate a stingingly inequitable dynamic—or worse, do those needs flat-out *create* it? The bottom line, it seems, is that despite your best intentions, the system is exploitive, and your very participation in it implicates you. Just in case you missed *how* potentially exploitive the system is, the book links the plight of nannies and maids with that of sex workers, and not altogether ludicrously: no matter how different their job descriptions, the prostitute and the nanny are both comfort providers offering a fleshy stock in trade; they are emotional proxies, trafficking in intimacy, that impossible-to-regulate thing.

Viewing the services supplied in stark industrial terms, the authors advance an unsavory analogy: "In an earlier phase of imperialism, northern countries extracted natural resources and agricultural products, rubber, metals, and sugar, for example, from lands they conquered and colonized. Today, while still relying on Third World countries for agricultural and industrial labor, the wealthy countries also seek to extract something harder to measure and quantify, something that can look very much like love."

Even more troubling, they go on to suggest, are the ostensible deficits and insufficiencies in us that have created the market for these emotion-based services: "It is as if the wealthy parts of the world are running short on precious emotional and sexual resources and have had to turn to poorer regions for fresh supplies."

So how does it play out in real life, in human terms, where dire need of one sort meets dire need of another?

"The illegal alien connection is a big deal here in Houston," says Maggie, a mother of twins. "You can imagine how divided our community is about that issue. Everybody pays lip service to the idea that we have to do something about illegal immigration, and then they start thinking it costs $35 to have their grass cut and $80 a day for a maid." When she was working full-time, Maggie's nanny, Marta, made about $18,000 under the table—manageable for Maggie, and enough for Marta to afford a decent apartment and a car in Texas. "When we lived in Washington, D.C., it was $150 a day for a maid, because she was legal. You feel bad perpetuating the system, but our nanny is twenty-nine, and she's been in this country since she was twelve. What are you gonna do, send her back to Mexico?"

But what is strangest about their relationship is the fact that over the seven years Marta has worked for Maggie, the question of her immigration status has never been brought up. She has requested her pay in cash, and conclusions could easily be drawn—the don't-ask-don't-tell approach is common enough when it comes to nannies.

And yet working in this country without papers is potentially punishable by deportation. Considering that one's children could be directly affected, wouldn't you think every conceivable question would be asked and answered concerning the background of the person providing the care, just as a pediatrician's qualifications are checked and vetted before he lays a hand on the little one? Why is avoidance and denial so rampant in the make-it-up-as-you-go universe of child care?

The year the big mirror got held up to the working mommy ranks was 1993, when President Clinton's pick for attorney general, Zoe Baird, withdrew her nomination after it was discovered she had hired an illegal immigrant to nanny her son, and neglected to pay taxes on her wages. Clinton's subsequent pick, Kimba Wood, withdrew her nomination after revealing that she'd also hired an undocumented worker, albeit before it had become illegal to do so (she'd even paid the appropriate payroll taxes). The feminists were in high dudgeon. The opposition had gone after Baird on this issue; why are

the child-care arrangements of a *male* nominee never scruti-
nized? And really, what's the big deal anyway? The women
were well treated and well compensated. And yet the
Baird/Wood double whammy cast a harsh light on the prac-
tice, revealing the unregulated dodginess of these arrangements, all of it unnecessary. As long as we're asking questions,
why was a very high-functioning, well-to-do woman like
Baird being less than thorough and up front about her child-
care?

To me it all reeked of ineffable ambivalence, on the personal level, certainly: if we were okay with going off to work
and leaving our children in the care of another, we would
treat her like a full-blown employee; we would make that financial, paperwork-laden commitment. We'd be out about it.
But we also feel society's ambivalence, from the minimal time
off granted new mothers by the corporations they work for,
to generally unsubsidized preschool and day care. The message sent to moms is *fend for yourself.*

From the benign local vantage of the home, it can be difficult to view one's relationship with one's smiling, confident,
affectionate nanny in exploitive political or socioeconomic
terms. We each have something the other needs, be it money
or skills, love and time; in the best sense of it, we make each
other's lives possible. And yet our points of reference, our perspective, our social spheres will always be worlds apart, as Hy
once pointed out to me in her typically dead-on way. Describing her job and how much she loves children, she once

said, "It's all about the kids. If it weren't for the kids, I wouldn't know you and you wouldn't know me."

As much as I wanted to argue that point with her, how ridiculous it would have been to try.

Hy, a twin, both the oldest of seven, gave up a job in Jamaica working as a cashier in a pastry shop to come here nineteen years ago, having heard so much about "the Big Apple." But she didn't have a visa, which meant going through Tijuana to California, where she was stopped by immigration, but easily got through when she and her fellow travelers said they were American. Then she spent three days in California, which was the scariest part; friends had arranged temporary lodging in a house where, she told me, there were drugs and guns. After that she came to New York. A Jamaican friend already working as a nanny invited her to stay at her place while she looked for a job. Hy got a taxi at La Guardia and was taken to the friend's address in Brooklyn.

At first it couldn't have been lonelier, sitting for days in the apartment with no job and no money. "When I first got here I started crying," Hy told me one day. "I wanted to go back home; I didn't like it here. Then I thought, what am I going to go back home to? I gave up my job. And I said, you know what? I'm gonna fight it out here. I'm not gonna give up." Besides, she said, "Everybody talks about America, America, America"—and she wanted to be part of it. She was the first of her sisters to come.

Eventually Hy got a child-care job with no experience beyond taking care of her own daughter (now grown and the mother of three). But she went out into the park, made friends, talked to people, and asked questions about where to take the kids, how to cure diaper rash, the best products to use. Given her conscientiousness and good nature, she turned into a pro. Now she's been in the business for almost two decades.

It would take years for me to learn even the basics of Hy's background, to say nothing of the nuances; a nanny reveals herself in the way she does her job. Befitting the murky nature of it, Hy's coming to us was a matter of happenstance and luck.

On one of those days when I was a wobbly new mom haunting the parks, I noticed a nanny taking beautiful care of her tiny charge, bouncing and tickling him, genuinely enjoying him. I sat down next to her, struck up a conversation, and asked what makes a good nanny—what should I be looking for? Her answers, if obvious, were sound: a caregiver needs to love children, the nanny told me—needs to have experience with them, needs to know how to make them happy, and so on.

Then I asked her if she knew anyone who was looking for a position. In fact she did: this friend of hers had a job that was ending because the family was moving to Westchester County. She'd be available in a couple of weeks, once she'd helped them relocate, the move being the thing bringing her job to an end. (*What a mensch. What dedication,* I thought.) Apparently, she'd be available right around the time I'd be needing someone. Her name was Hy.

I remember the first time we talked on the phone: When I complimented her on her lovely surname, her curt "Thank you" told me she'd heard this before from my kind; let's cut the small talk and get down to business. We arranged to meet.

As you might recall, Hy wasn't in the house a full minute before taking control of my kid, so there was never any awkward handing over of the baby. In moments she had my girl, now awake, laid out on her back in Hy's two hands—one under her butt, one under her upper back—a fan of long fingers supporting her head and neck. Sophie was staring into her large, dark eyes now, her mouth twisting into a smile as Hy cooed and shook her head from side to side, rattling her big gold hoop earrings. For Sophie to be awake and not crying while *not* drunk on milk was a new one on me; I knew I was in the presence of a professional.

I asked Hy about her previous jobs; of course I'd be calling her references, for what that's worth, although I wanted to know how she'd felt about them. And I was all but sold when she told me she'd worked for a time as an attendant to the elderly, which she didn't enjoy as much as working with kids. Why? "Because you can love up a baby," as she put it. "It's not so easy to love and hug up an old person." I hadn't thought of it before, but I pretty much knew what she meant. I loved that response. That's what I was looking for—someone to love up my kid.

She also told me how important it was for her to work with

a *nice* family; in fact, she said this more than once. And I couldn't help but wonder what rotten treatment she'd suffered in the past to make mere niceness such a high priority.

I hired her, provisionally. As the end of my maternity leave pulled into view, I knew it was time to administer the real test: leaving Hy alone with the baby. So I cooked up an errand that would take a couple of hours, and I can still recall that sensation of rubber-legged disorientation as I left our building and walked into the sun alone, no Bjorn strapped to my chest, no hummingbird heartbeat contrapuntal to mine. I had such a clear sense of having been transformed: I was a different person on the most organic level, someone not entirely myself when this other little piece of me was somewhere else. Walking up the block I felt cosmically unmoored.

I called several times during the course of the errand. Hy expected it and kindly gave me what I needed, which was lots of information about this uneventful interlude—the banana slice consumed, the excrement produced. In spite of my anxiety, when I returned, the baby was gurgling, thoroughly intact.

In those early weeks, Hy exuded remarkable competence, and that meant a lot to me. Appropriately, she was far more focused on the baby than on us; our relationship, hers and mine, was nebulous. In the interview she'd been more nervous than warm, a little stiff, maybe, with an irksome habit of introducing answers to my questions with "I'm not gonna lie to you," as if lying were an option. (I would later learn that this is more of a verbal tic than anything—one I've grown quite fond of.)

I didn't anticipate great closeness between us. *But that's okay,* I thought; *it's more about the baby than me,* not yet sensing the deep, sweet, roiling emotion in Hy that would come to envelop us all.

OH SWEET MYSTERY OF LIFE
AT LAST I'VE FOUND YOU

"**S**HE IS SO perfect that I don't feel like we're perfect enough for her. I'm learning everything from her—she's taught me how to take care of my baby. From the way she cuts a grilled cheese sandwich to the way she cleans my sink and leaves a washcloth hanging to dry, everything she does is really artful and lovely. Everything is done in a nice, caring, beautiful way. We live like we never lived before we had children. We didn't have food, we didn't have a stack of toilet paper rolls and paper towels and aluminum foil; she's taught me how to run a household. She is perfect."

So says Jill, mother of Emma, sixteen months old. She is talking about Gloria, the Jamaican nanny who has been with them from the start. You encounter this sort of ecstatic effusion frequently among mothers of very small children, for whom the nanny phenomenon is still a novelty. Of course, who wouldn't be grateful for skilled and efficient assistance during that chaotic time when bodily functions and fluids rule your life?

But there's something else, I think. The abject gratitude heaped upon nannies in the beginning has at least as much to do with the fact that so many urban professional women don't live anywhere near their mothers, aunts, or sisters anymore; our families tend to be discrete little units rooted in places rich with jobs. We haven't been schooled in the arcane traditions and customs of motherhood. We don't know the wives' tales, we don't know the miracle cures, we don't even know the lullabies. When we pop out that kid during a brief lull in the career climb, we're pretty much on our own. The reasonable notion that it takes a village to raise a child is greatly complicated by the fact that we don't live in villages anymore. So we hire someone to come and be part of our village.

And she knows it all, she's the shaman—the one who shows us the proper angle at which to hold the bottle, the best method for burping (a circular fingertip massage interspersed with tender pats on the back between the tiny, winglike shoulder blades), the fail-safe technique for thermometer insertion (a slow, gentle twist, aided by a dab of Vaseline), the best product for a chapped behind (A & D ointment, not cream—Triple Paste if it's serious). "She taught me that when my son had a stuffed nose, I was supposed to put pepper under it so he would sneeze and all the gunk would finally come out," Elena, a Washington, D.C.-area mom, told me, still awed five years later by the ingeniousness of that.

"She taught me all the little things, like how to clean his

78

bottom and get in all the creases," says another. "I didn't even think about those things."

Your nanny knows before you do about the variety of shrieks and cries, the one that means hunger, the one that means wetness, the one that means *Please put me in my crib.* She can tell how well the baby has eaten merely by hoisting him like a Christmas ham. "You feel the weight on him, Mommy?" she'll say with a smile, as heartened as you are by evidence that he's thriving.

She's confident, unflappable, brimming with indispensable folk wisdom. The baby has an especially dark web of veins under his tongue? He'll be an early talker. He's got infant acne on his cheeks? Drag a wet diaper across them. (I have yet to find a pediatrician, or dermatologist, or urologist who can confirm the efficacy of this one.) The plants are greener and lusher than usual? There's new life in the house; in other words, Mommy is pregnant with number two. (Damned if Hy didn't call it.)

She is magical, just like in the movies. As with Mary Poppins or Nanny McPhee or even Mrs. Doubtfire, her efficient rounds should be accompanied by some winsomely witchy soundtrack, some Danny Elfman–ish testament to her supernatural charms.

Her impact is unquantifiable. How odd and funny my husband and I thought it was when our baby would laugh and shake her head in the high chair as we tried to feed her tiny spoonfuls of something pasty, until we realized this is what Hy does with her: she shakes her head, delighting the baby with the clank of her earrings (causing the baby's lips to joyfully part and thus provide an opening for the food). In those early days, how Sophie would scream with glee when we would open the door in the morning to find no one there until a second later, when a grinning Hy would roll rakishly into view from behind the door. At the end of the day, as she prepared to leave, slipping on her street shoes and rubbing her hands with lotion, she'd temper Sophie's panic and sadness with the utterance of one word—"Tomorrow"—with tender finality and the iron-clad sense of promise that she would return.

In some of the very best ways, she was everything I wasn't. Hy was spontaneous; I was ruminative. She was lacquered and curvaceous and Bedazzled; I was hipless and mannish and black-clad. She was butter-fried chicken cutlets that perfumed the house; I was tofu and broccoli. She was focused; I was distracted. And that pleased me more than it gave me pause. Our love affair with Hy was officially under way.

The new nanny feels like family. But her appeal isn't only about the tutorial in nurture the modern, deracinated new mom is so happy to receive. It's also about the wholly unanticipated fact that the mother is deriving some nurture from this arrangement as well.

This woman arrives at a time of extreme vulnerability, as Mom attempts to heal and somehow ride an emotional mudslide. As the nanny pitches in with her calm skill and care, she feels like a motherly figure to *us*. She all but promises to make everything okay, which, as can-do women driven to make something of ourselves, we haven't asked of our own mothers since childhood. For good or ill, neediness is something we long ago attempted to shed.

One time when I came home from a truly punishing day at work to find Hy ministering to the kids so gently, I had an urge I couldn't resist: to take a hug from her—and that's what if felt like, taking—to get some of that loving action for my-self. As I nestled in on her with a groan about the day, she laughed and gave me a sisterly pat. What else could she do? I'd pretty much forced myself on her. No great harm done, but her job is with the children. Reflecting on the incident, I feel like I'd crossed the line.

ANSWERED PRAYERS

As the nervousness that comes with building a new relation-ship and having a stranger in your home gives way to unimag-inable familiarity, you can't help but take pleasure in the signs of progress—reveling in the sight of your baby passed out on your nanny's bosom shelf, ragdoll arms draped over her shoul-der, eyelids fluttering, her mouth a tiny "o" as your nanny coos and rubs her back. Meanwhile, the baby's room looks like a spread from *Child* magazine: the crib sheet taut, the stuffed animals lined up, the little T-shirts and Onesies folded just so, thanks to the consummate professional who's in charge and cannot abide disarray. No matter how closely you study her moves and attempt to replicate her level of pressed and tucked and spit-polished efficiency on those rare occasions when she's not around, the place just doesn't look the same when you're done with it. In all sorts of ways, you've never had it so good.

Many a new mother is happy to give herself over to the arrangement: that willful surrender to the wisdom and judgment of a woman she hardly knows is a reflection of her desire for it all to be true, that she *is* a miracle—"the Jamaican Mary Poppins," as one mother proudly describes the woman she hired—and that this arrangement is actually working out great, the best decision she could have made. *Not only is nothing lost by my going back to work; my kid's got it even better than if I'd stayed home. It's almost as if she's got three parents instead of two!* That's a lovely idea.

And on some level it *is* the best thing that ever happened to us. For a stranger to take on our chaos and our challenges so cheerfully is, by any measure, a wondrous thing. And the gratitude we feel has a way of transmogrifying into something akin to romantic love. "If she ever left us, I'd kill myself," many a besotted new mom has said.

Perhaps a whiff of romance is inevitable with any relationship as intimate and symbiotic as this one, as marriagelike as it frequently seems. "She's my husband," one woman, the wife of an overworked lawyer, said to me, simply. "She allowed me to get divorced," says another. Meaning, without the nanny's support, going it alone would have been unthinkable.

I've heard countless iterations of the marital analogy in reference to the partnership that takes shape, given the household rituals and routines that bind them in this shared project: the nanny calling the mother to remind her to pick up diapers and formula; the mother calling the nanny to check in—the nanny putting the phone to the baby's drooling lips so Mom can hear her, and feel connected, in exactly the same way stay-at-home mothers do for their office-bound husbands. On occasion, I've even gotten so girlie—let's say wifely—with Hy that I've asked her with a shriek to please dispatch a largish bug in the bathroom; once I implored her to remove and flush a dead fish from the tank (granted, I had my hands full with the crying child who'd discovered the corpse). And no, I'm not proud of that; I worry it violates a commandment that ought to be needlepointed and framed on all our walls: *Never ask your nanny to do anything you wouldn't do yourself.* That said, fair or not, I sometimes count on her to be bigger, stronger, better than I am.

The temptation is hard to resist. What power to be able to say so casually, "Please take so-and-so to a playdate," on the East Side about twenty blocks down that will require an umbrella, a bus transfer, and the collapsing and hauling of a stroller under one arm, the squirming child under the other. Please also sit there for the duration of the playdate with the child's dreary mother—potentially three hours or more—something you're utterly unwilling to do yourself. Knowing there's someone there to fetch the juice, to wipe the runny nose, you can find yourself growing shockingly lazy. What an exploitable pleasure it is to know that if your kid pees in his bed or pukes all over everything, the mess will magically disappear in the morning, once the nanny arrives. *Not your problem.*

"One weekend the parents got stuck in New York, so I was with the girls," says Abby from South Carolina, who worked for a wealthy family in Los Angeles during college and a few years after. "And there were six kids coming over to spend the night, and the parents knew I'd be fine. I had to talk to all the other mothers and let them know I felt very confident about having their daughters over. So I had to bring them all home from the soccer game. I drove the Volvo station wagon, like a soccer mom, and gave them dinner, made sure one of them took her medicine, got them all to sleep, and got them up in the morning for another soccer game." Abby smiles. "I was twenty-two," she says, laughing now and looking a little dazed as she thinks back on the amount of responsibility she was expected to shoulder. "Isn't that funny?"

It's an exhausting job you ask a nanny to do, which comes with unimaginable new twists and demands every day. But is there a breaking point? How close is she to it? You'll never know until she gets there.

Mothers—especially the overeducated, overthinking older ones—can be a handful for even the most phlegmatic nanny. "I was totally freaked out," says Elena, who was the ripe old age of forty-three when she had her son. "I was overwhelmed, totally a nut, thinking everything I did or didn't do was gonna ruin the kid's life—I was sure he would die at any moment." Blessedly self-aware at this point, she is the first to admit that her efforts to stave off disaster included micro-analysis and overmanagement. "I did everything recommended in all the books I'd bought and researched, because I approached child rearing like I did my job and everything else I had done in my life, which was to study and become an expert, so to speak. Obviously, in this case that didn't work."

Once her Guatemalan nanny, Gabriella, arrived, it only got worse. "I immediately went into my one millionth tailspin, where I think my child will no longer think I'm his mother, that he's now only going to love Gabriella." She heaves a sigh at her own expense. "That was a complete emotional nightmare for me. I was a basket case, calling home every fifteen minutes. I was horrible. I'm sure Gabriella hated us in the beginning."

People—women—are who they are, although I suspect the fact that Elena had her son relatively late in life might have contributed to her difficulties. Anyone who waits that long to become a parent, and knows this is the only child she's going to have, isn't likely to hand him over without a fight.

Elena got ahold of herself eventually, growing happily dependent on the intuitive, skillful Gabriella. In the best of worlds, mothers aren't so ambivalent and conflicted that they can't allow nannies to become partners in this critical project—to become emotionally invested. When Sophie was a few months old, I well remember Hy and me standing side by side at her changing table and examining the mustardy stool in the baby's diaper. As Sophie lay there clueless and nude, both of us were very pleased to note that the stool was firmer than it had been the past few days. In fact, if memory serves, I think we may have even exchanged a high-five; clearly, Hy had been as concerned as I was.

When my son, Owen, who came three years after Sophie, was a year or so old, I recall Hy's motherly indignation when some visitor commented that he seemed to be a little on the smallish side for his age. "Yes," she retorted, "but he's very *flexible!*" She was as proud and protective of my kids, as quick as I was to brag and defend; how incensed she was when one of our children was wait-listed at a preschool—the nerve of them not rushing to accept the most perfect child in the world! It told me a lot about the level of her commitment.

Linda, a New York lawyer, tells me about Seena, nanny to her two sons, who has always been sensitive to one of the boys' learning issues. "With someone else," Linda says, "maybe they'd be judgmental, or it would impact how she felt about him. But she was very supportive and caring." At a certain point when he was struggling in school, the family considered making a change, and Seena weighed in. " 'I think he would do better somewhere else,' " Linda recalls her saying. Then Linda wells up: "When we found another school, she visited it herself and said, 'I really like it. I think he'll be happy there.' " That degree of attention and care meant everything.

Joy, disappointment, intense loyalty, and tears can find their way into anyone's nine-to-five. But when nannies show emotion, we take it as evidence that this, in fact, is far more than a job to her. One day we were horrified to come home and find our impressively put-together, stoic Hy sitting on a chair, in tears. After much pleading and cajoling, she told us what had happened. Apparently, our two-year-old was saying he didn't like her. "This has never happened to me before with any child I've ever worked with, and I don't like it," she said between sobs, wiping her eyes with a balled-up tissue.

Now this was inconceivable; our son laughed and smiled incessantly in her presence, and asked about her throughout the weekend. It took awhile, but I finally untangled the mystery: his older sister had lately been spouting a singsongy favorite of the kid crowd since time immemorial. "I don't *like* you," they say, watching your face fall theatrically, only to perk you back up with, "I *love* you!" Unfortunately, our then language-challenged two-year-old, not yet capable of complete sentences, had only mastered the first half (he'd been doing the same thing with us over the last few days). In a rush of relief I explained it all to Hy, and she got it, quickly drying her tears. I don't ever want to see her cry again, but it was astonishing to realize how easily she could be hurt by us, how emotionally involved she was with our children, and how reassuring that felt.

It stands to reason, I suppose, that this job would entail this level of feeling. You don't feed, cuddle, laugh with, and comfort a child every day for years without it having an impact. If you've had a close relationship with a nanny, you know this in your heart. So it can be strange when outsiders patently don't get it. In July of 2005 the *New York Times* ran an article that carried the headline "City Nannies Say They, Too, Can Be Mother Lions": "It bewildered some rescue workers on Thursday to realize that the tiny child buried beneath the rubble of a building that had just collapsed on Broadway, the one Brunilda Tirado had been calling for desperately—'My baby! My baby!'—was not Ms. Tirado's child at all. But scores of her fellow nannies, who spend their days caring for other people's children, were surprised by the surprise."

The article also harkens back to a harrowing scene that occurred over a decade ago, when "a 19-month-old girl was killed and her baby sitter lost a leg trying to save the girl from an out-of-control car that jumped the curb," not far from the incident involving Ms. Tirado. "We didn't make them," a nanny is quoted in the article as saying about the children they care for so selflessly. "But they're ours and we love them dearly, dearly." I know this to be true. It makes me want to laminate the article and stick it under the noses of the legion of skeptics roaming around out there.

A year later came another round of local headlines about a baby who'd been choking on a chunk of fruit. As the story went, his nanny scooped him up and was running with him as he turned blue in her arms when they were hit by a van. A cop fetched the child and got him to the hospital, while the nanny sustained serious injury to one of her legs. Both she and the child are okay now. Inevitably, another mother tried to hire her away—what mom doesn't fantasize about someone who'd risk her own life for their kid?

MAKING A COMMITMENT

The potential for emotional entanglement and dependency between mother and nanny is so great, it doesn't surprise me that many moms just aren't up for it—maybe even fear it— defaulting instead to the revolving-door approach. They bring on women and for one reason or another let them go in a matter of months. The littlest things will set them off—the nanny is late, talked back, left the baby's room untidy. Yes, it's an incredibly important hire, and perfection is the goal. But with some of these mothers, it's almost as if they have the kind of "intimacy issues" one associates with serial daters. You can skirt the pressure of having to get close if the person isn't around long enough for closeness to be possible. And with a revolving-door nanny, there is no threat of the children growing too attached.

Mothers can also find themselves confronting a Fellini-esque cast of caregivers when they haven't sufficiently thought out their needs, when their arrangements are basically cobbled together. Again, denial is a factor; when the hours you require coverage are always in flux, you needn't say with certainty, "Yes, I've gone back to work; I've made that choice, and I'm

reliant on someone to help me make that happen." No commitments, no attachments, keep it fuzzy; it's a hard way to live,
although some mothers prefer it like that.

Mary, a smart, vigilant, professional type with a good sense
of humor about child-care-related foibles, tells me about the
weirdly haphazard arrangements she put together for her son.
"I had one woman who worked for us for a while and then
sort of started pulling in people she knew," she says. "She was
like, 'Oh, I can't come at that time, but my friend babysits.'
And I'd think, *You're kind of working out; I'm a little scared of
you, but you're kind of working out, so maybe your friend will work
out.* And then they'd switch shifts on me and I'd expect Freda
to be there and Jane would show up, or I'd open up the door
and it would be someone else . . . I'd need to be at a client's
by 8:00 and it would be 7:30, and no one would be there. It
was a lot of stress. It was like, open the door and find your
mystery date! Every day! I'd be all dressed, all ready to go to
work and open the door—who is it today?"

The alternative is to give yourself over, to enter into a partnership that grows intimate almost instantly. When she arrives,
you're in your nightgown. Soon she'll be seeing you fresh from
the shower. She can tell when you're dieting, she'll see the un-
paid bills pile up, she'll know when you and your husband are
fighting, she'll see you cry. On Monday morning, she'll see one
wine or beer bottle too many in the recycle bin—and not say a
word. She'll sense how close to a breakdown you really are,
having caught you madly flipping through infant care guides

and consulting specialists when you thought your baby's thousand-yard stare surely meant he had some seizure-inducing neurological disorder. She's got your number.

If you live in a city and your space is limited, on the nights your nanny winds up sleeping over it'll be on a fold-out couch in the middle of the living room. And yes, you'll see her in her PJs, too. In the morning your boundary-oblivious kids, thrilled to have access to her so early in the day, will dive in for a snuggle, happily tangling in her nightgown and fingering her ankle bracelet, tracing her polished toenails while chattering away about the day ahead—you cannot put a price on the sweetness of that. And yet what employee in any other field finds herself in that position, where the lines are that fungible? This is her place of business, after all.

One of the reasons I'll always drag myself into the office, no matter how poorly I'm feeling, is that I recognize our home is Hy's daytime domain. Her having to work around me all laid up in bed would be like my boss parking her rear on my keyboard for the day and me trying to type around her.

The intimacy fostered is such that really good nannies are sensitive to the organic, ever-changing nature of the relationships in the family; indeed, the moods and well-being of the parents directly affect her charges, her job. One morning Hy instructed me to kiss my husband before I left for work; it was a rough time full of distractions, and I clearly didn't have it in me that day to make it happen on my own. To be sure, it was a cheeky suggestion on her part, ostensibly outside her purview, but I got it. If he and I aren't a smooth, fully functioning unit, we're all in trouble.

Like a shareholder's report, a couple's relationship on any given day tells her something about the health and stability of the firm that employs her. "She had to deal with arguments at times," one corporate executive says of her nanny, a miracle-worker from the West Indies. "Then my husband was sleeping on the couch for a few months. Then he moved out. So it was just very tense." Eventually the couple divorced, and the nanny all but became this woman's husband.

"She takes care of everything, every single thing," the mom says. "She does errands, whether it's waiting for the cable guy or buying lightbulbs and toothpaste, or picking up the dry cleaning, or this pot my kid painted; getting my daughter to piano and my son to gymnastics. She does everything so that I can focus on work and do better financially, so I can try to maintain the same kind of lifestyle for my kids, so I can give them a family life that's as close as possible to what we had before. And because of her, when I come home at night, all I have to do is spend time with my kids.

"I am so grateful," she says. "I could not do it without her. And *her*—in particular. She really, really goes above and beyond and puts up with a lot: going to my ex-husband's house some mornings at 6:30 in the morning to take over with the kids, driving stuff back and forth. We are *not* easy people to work for. The situation isn't easy. And a lot of people would say, 'The hell with that.'"

By way of thanks, the mom regularly gives the nanny things like plane tickets to Europe, a laptop, Broadway tickets. "Anything I can do for her," she says, "I do without question."

You are a team. The synergy between you is unlike anything you've experienced before. This occurred to me one day when I pulled back and took a good clinical look at my life at the time, specifically at how I fed my baby. Every morning as I headed for the elevator, Hy loaded me up with my various bags, leaving the heavy, clumsy breast pump for last. Then off I'd go to my office at a magazine where the staff was approximately 90 percent male. About three times a day I'd slide shut my frosted glass door and fire up the pump, holding a plastic funnel to my naked breast as it sucked milk down the tube and into a bottle—this while guys threw a football and talked about girls' outfits and asses right outside my door. To aid in milk production, I'd stare at a framed picture of my son on my desk, the sight of those chubby cheeks provoking "letdown."

When I came home in the evening, the first order of business would be to unpack the freezer bag containing the milk I'd produced. Hy would be there, praising me if there was a lot, grimacing if there wasn't (surreally, my milk production specifically impacted her ability to do her job well). Then she would hold open a Ziploc bag into which I'd pour the milk from a plastic bottle, shaking out the last drop before she closed up the bag and stowed it in the freezer for the following day. If it looked like we'd be short, she would encourage me to retreat to the bedroom and try to pump a little more. Then I'd pour the extra into the Baggie she held—her hands literally filling with my still-warm milk.

Now let's review: I go to work at least partly so that we can afford Hy, whose job it is to feed my son. And what she feeds him is something only I can produce. This I'll do behind the closed door of a sterile office thirty blocks away while staring not at my son but a framed picture of him, while attached to a machine that simulates his sucking. The yield goes from breast to storage bottle to Hy to baby bottle to my son. All in all, it seemed a ludicrously convoluted way to get him fed, but here we are.

This much I realized: as far as feeding my child was concerned, the job required us both. Together, we equaled one superefficient mom.

GETTING TO KNOW YOU

During the honeymoon period, we are so dependent on our nannies that any potential for discord is glossed over with gratitude. To be sure, there is a period where even if she exhibited flaws, we wouldn't be able to see them.

"I've never had a complaint about anything she's done for my child. I never worry about her safety," the head-over-heels Jill continues. "She loves my child as if she were her own. Honest to God. Loves her, worships her, adores her. The love is so true."

As I listen, I realize how churlish it would be to ask Jill how she knows this to be the case. Although when she tells me that "all the other nannies at the playground gossip about the families they work for, but Gloria doesn't, she sits alone," I can't resist. "How do I know?" she says. "She told me herself."

The need to believe she is perfect is so strong that almost anything can be overlooked, forgiven, explained. Consider this one: "One day Adriana said to me, 'Mama, can I see your pussy?'" Debra's eyes grow wide telling me this; she is able to muster a throaty chuckle recalling this uniquely touchy situation. "My jaw was on the floor. But I didn't want to make too big a deal about it. I said, 'Where did you learn that word?' And she said 'Ginger'—our babysitter. And I said, 'Really?' She said, 'Yes.' And she started saying it again and again, and then her big sister started saying it and they're hysterical about it." Understand that in every other way Debra regarded Ginger as the Rolls Royce of nannies: attentive, intuitive, reliable, warm.

"So the next day I asked Ginger about it. I said, 'The girls are using this word,' and I spelled it out. And she goes 'Oh!'— a little bemused. Then she said she'd been telling them the story of Puss 'N Boots, and that's where they must have gotten it."

In the telling, Debra didn't seem especially convinced, although neither was she willing to read any real darkness or irresponsibility into it. "Part of me thinks it's kind of funny, and they're probably hearing a lot worse than this. You have to meet Ginger to know she's a very maternal woman, whom I can't imagine would do anything inappropriate. She's from Guyana, and part of me thought maybe it's a word that's meaningless in Guyana. But it was a little freaky. She knew; she was embarrassed."

Maybe it was nothing. A nasty word slipping in from time to time, the verbal equivalent, arguably, of occasionally giving the kids junk food and parking them in front of crap TV now and then. Not ideal, but not a crime. And when you've put your trust in someone the way you do a babysitter, there is a limit to how much you can and should police her. But still . . .

In the early stages of any romance, the parties involved are overly polite with each other, taking care not to overstep. But in the case of mothers and nannies, it's the mothers who go to almost comic lengths to keep things upbeat—copacetic. One Caribbean nanny had a very tough time pronouncing the first name of the man whose children she'd just begun taking care of. But rather than correct her, neither mother nor father said anything, so unwilling were they to risk embarrassing the beloved nanny in any way. Ultimately, the nanny dealt with the problem by simply referring to him as the children did—Daddy.

Janine, who lives in Westchester with her husband and two daughters, was faced with a similarly awkward situation. "Gayle would keep this log of what Samantha ate all day for me, and how she would sleep and for how long, which I loved," she says. "And when I came home, I'd read it. But when she wrote 'bowl,' she'd spell it 'blow.' Every time. And it would drive my husband crazy. So I told him, 'I should just do her a favor and say, 'This is how you spell *bowl*.' And he was like, you can't do that; that's crossing the line. She'll be insulted. And I said, 'I'm gonna do it.'

"So one day I said to Gayle, 'Know what? I'm an editor, so I know this stuff, and I can't help myself, but you spell "bowl" this way.' And she was like, 'Well, in *my* country, we spell it *this* way.' And then I felt awful. I think I made her feel stupid, and she had to come up with that excuse. And so I've never done it again. I had these fantasies that I'd do her a favor and sit down and tutor her, but it's never going to happen."

There's awareness all around that we're engaged in the most important job there is, that we're asking this woman to safeguard our kids in the most fundamental way; in that context it feels foolish to sweat the little things. Or, we worry, if we annoy the nanny by splitting hairs, could that poison her relationship with the child? Might she take her frustration out on him? When you're asking this person to keep your kid from harm's way and make him smile, where do you find the space in your relationship to make an issue of things like spelling and which brand of hand soap to buy, and the fact that after unpacking the groceries, you'd prefer it if she'd pull the paper shopping bag from the plastic one and fold them neatly along their seams before putting them away?

For me, an early test of this kind came with the question of how Hy was going to address me. From the first day she started calling me "Miss Lucy," which made me uncomfortable, with the images it conjured of plantation-style servitude. So one evening I said to her, "You really don't have to call me that; Lucy's fine." I felt good about that display of bleeding-heart largesse. But Hy just smiled, a little slyly, I think, and went right on calling me Miss Lucy.

So here was a conundrum: do I allow it to continue, wincing every time anyone overhears it, worrying about the message it sends to my kids? Or do I pull rank—that is, big-foot her, boss-lady style—and insist she address me the way a compassionate liberal prefers to be addressed? I let it drop, leaving Hy to do what apparently made her comfortable, and took it as a victory when she eventually shortened it to the more affectionate-sounding "Miss Luce" or "Miss Lu."

In a way I was trying to bridge the cultural divide. But I was also trying to humanize the situation, to make it clear, however ham-fistedly, that she was more than a mere employee to me. It wouldn't be the last time, and I wasn't alone. Once she came on board, I noticed us playing a lot of Bob Marley around the house. Any chance we got, we talked up the Jamaican hero with Hy. Was she a fan? Did she ever see him perform? We'd say what a great CD *Legend* is. Then one day Hy remarked what a coincidence it was that a former boss of hers was also a big Bob Marley fan; he talked about him, played him all the time. And in that moment, I thought, *that guy was going through exactly what we are—doing his best to reach out, connect, and be respectful of this all-important stranger in his midst.*

WHO'S THE MOTHER?

In the first few months, the contentedly clueless infant is perfectly happy with whatever set of helping hands comes his way. And if the hands belong to a nanny, the sticky, gurgling lovebug can be a tad oblique when that other woman shows up around six—the one who resembles him, who rushes toward him and scoops him up rather greedily. If he's strapped into his stroller, just back from the park, the good nanny behind him will roll the stroller onto its back wheels, allowing the mom's lips better access to his face—the nanny knows that's job one, facilitating the high-stakes reunion kiss. And yes, the baby will smile, but then possibly look away, still ensconced in his day with this other mom figure.

Which raises the question, where else in your life does the success of your endeavors threaten to erode your self-esteem? "For a while, when I would walk in, Emma wanted to stay with Gloria if Gloria was holding her, and that was hard, a little bit," Jill tells me. "But I didn't get overly distraught; I knew Emma was like an amoeba, and she was just happy being in the warm arms of whoever was holding her. And I love that she loves Gloria. If she runs to her, or if she cries when she leaves, I don't mind. I just never have worried for one second in the world with her. Everyone has said, 'Do you know how lucky you are?' Everyone can see that it's not a nanny, it's another mother."

On some level it sounds like a brave front, and why not?

There is no percentage in indulging insecurities. For a period of time this woman is her right arm; no good can come of alienating her.

There are aspects of this job that threaten to literally fuse mother and nanny. When it's time to cut the baby's toenails, one of you will hold the aphidlike digits while the other wields the clippers, the two of you toiling in a workspace the size of a dollhouse dessert plate. When medicine is called for, one will gently steady the puling face with forefinger and thumb while the other guides the liquid on a spoon down the hatch. When the baby bumps his head and cries, it will happen time and again that you both reach for him at once, your hands colliding as they simultaneously go to rub the bruise. If you get to the baby first, he'll wail and reach for the nanny; if she gets their first, he'll twist and go for you. And she will relinquish him if she's smart.

One mother describes the curious dance that ensues when they take her little one to the doctor for a shot: as the needle comes out, the child crawls into the nanny's lap; when the cruel deed is done and the child starts to cry, she climbs back to Mommy. One day I showed up unannounced at a toddler class that Owen always attended with Hy. How whipsawed he was by my presence—whom should he toss the ball to, whom should he play the hand-clapping game with, me or his regular partner, Hy? We did the best we could, enlarging the circle to accommodate three. I'm afraid the whole experience was more befuddling for him than fun.

Indeed, for a tiny soul concerned primarily with survival, the mother-nanny overlap, and occasional interchangeability, can be difficult to sort out. "Mama, did I come out of Ginger's tummy?" asked Debra's younger daughter one day. To her credit, I guess, Debra just laughs it off. Any and all indications that the bond between them is strong are taken by her as positive signs. According to Debra, she never feels jealous.

"Sometimes the girls will say, 'I love Ginger more than you,' or "I miss Ginger,' or 'I'm gonna tell Ginger . . .' And it makes me happy." Not jumping-up-and-down happy, I suspect. But as mothers, we're grateful for our children to have these additional sources of comfort, these signs that something loving and good is happening when we're not there. I am reminded of young Harriet in Louise Fitzhugh's smart, moody novel about a solitary New York rich kid, *Harriet the Spy*, who in times of stress repeats like a mantra: "Ole Golly, Ole Golly, Ole Golly . . . ," the name of her nanny.

In short order, they are under our skin and in our lives, integral players in the daily routine. My in-laws are traditional types; back in the sixties and seventies, my husband's mother spent the better part of every day loading up the station wagon with groceries, sewing patches on torn trousers, and ferrying her four boys to one athletic meet or another in the Jersey suburbs, while her husband did hard time after work as a scoutmaster. Nannies were decidedly not in the picture.

And so, as you might imagine, it didn't go over well when my husband's parents caught our daughter, not yet two, referring to Hy as "Mama." Uncharacteristically, these circumspect people couldn't help but one day say out loud something to the effect of "That's not right."

There was nothing I could do. I'd basically asked Hy to be a surrogate mother; "Mommy" was pretty much the proper appellation, for the time being, a sign that everything was going according to plan. My old-school in-laws had to trust us on this one. Difficult as it was, and to their great credit, they ultimately did. Now, with a certain pro forma respect, they make a point of asking about Hy when we visit (even though I suspect they'll never be completely adjusted to the arrangement).

A NANNY'S REACH

She works her way into the fabric of a family in wholly unanticipated ways. Not only will your nanny guide your child's social life through the connections they make in the park and at school, but to a large extent she'll also influence yours. A mother called me out of the blue one day: "Hey, our children play together every day, and our nannies have become best friends. Maybe we should meet." Our families ended up sharing a summer house for years, all because of the nannies.

Four decades after Florence made her indelible impression on me—with her stories about growing up in Alabama, about running through the woods with her brothers and cutting open snakes to free the as-yet-undigested bunnies inside;

about having twin brothers twenty-six years younger than she; about marrying a man more than a foot taller and having to stand on a box while exchanging vows; about not being able to have children of her own—I'm still folding shirts the way she taught me: in lengthwise thirds, the sleeves tucked just so. And now I'm teaching my daughter the same method. Not exactly character-forming folk wisdom, but there's something about the continuity of that, the connection running between a little girl and a woman she'll never know, who had a lot to do with making her mom who she is—that strikes me as being valuable beyond measure.

Florence was onto it, I think. She was uncannily intuitive and clever; for instance, managing my fear of houseflies by encouraging me to name them (there's Frank; there's Zsa Zsa; hey Jerome, get off my toast). Several years after she left us, we visited her in New Jersey, an exhilarating reunion with one of the best people any of us had ever known. What a surprise it was to see her in her own small, comfortable home, as we'd only ever known her in ours.

She gave us the house tour; it was typical Florence wit that when guests were over, she stashed dirty plates in the washing machine as though it were a dishwasher, something she didn't own. And when we got to her bedroom, she pulled open the top bureau drawer to show us a small stack of Carter's infant T-shirts, neatly folded in lengthwise thirds. Our T-shirts, which she had taken as keepsakes when she left us. My sister and I, teenagers at the time of the visit, were gratified to think that she was as sentimental about our time together as we were. (As it happened, a major snowstorm hit New Jersey that day—a bonus, a big gift for my sister and me because we all had to stay over an extra night. It would be the last time we ever saw Florence.)

The impact a nanny has on a child could never be quantified or fully fathomed. As a force in your life she hovers somewhere between employee and blood relative, between stranger and the person you trust most in the world. During the first-blush, besotted early days with Hy, I frequently fantasized that if my husband and I were suddenly to go up in a ball of flame, she'd in some ways be the best guardian for Sophie, given her almost cellular level of familiarity with her needs—this despite the cultural differences and the patent perfection of my sister for that role.

While that musing was little more than a morbid what-if, typical of overstimulated new moms, my beyond-the-call-of-duty faith in Hy has always been profound. One day it was actually put to the test, when the Twin Towers fell less than five miles from our home. My best friend's wedding was taking place in a suburb of Massachusetts four days later. We had plane tickets for the whole family. Devastated and frightened, we came close to not going, although even as chaos reigned and toxic clouds of smoke wafted through the city, I knew I had to try; I was the matron of honor, and I had every reason to pull out the stops for this particular friend. Of course air travel was out of the question, so we arranged for a rental car. Several hours on the road on one of the most stressful Fridays in American history—I didn't feel good about subjecting the children to that. But leave them in the literally smoldering wreckage of New York, a quick trip from the heart of the horror? We were just days past the attack—who knew what lay ahead? Who knew if it was even over? Would it be safe here?

Maybe this sounds crazy to a non–New Yorker, or to someone who's never employed a nanny she loved and trusted utterly, but we decided to ask Hy to stay with them in the city for the weekend. That our guts told us the children would be better off at home with her in New York than on the road with us during that terrible time said it all about our bond, our indescribable faith in Hy. (Of course the children had a fine, fun, treats-and-videos-filled weekend, thanks partly to their obliviousness to what had happened downtown.)

She has your life in her hands; she'll make an almost mystical impact. All of us who employ women from the Caribbean note at a certain point that our children start to sound like them: accenting the first syllable of "museum," calling the faucet a "pipe" and the washcloth a "rag," much of it said with a musical lilt. The nanny's influence runs deep: she'll affect the way your child behaves, sees the world, expresses himself. And there is no end of factors that will determine your reaction to that.

WHO'S THE BOSS?

Although I'd never be entirely comfortable with Hy address-
ing me as Miss Lucy, I had to get over it. When I asked her
about it again years later, she simply told me that's what she is
used to. But I also think there's a sense in which it clarified
our roles in her mind, and I understand the value of that.
Nannies today encounter a lot of well-meaning white employers who aren't comfortable being bosses. So instead they
speak of the nanny as working *with* us, not *for* us; they insist
that the nanny is part of *our family*. And while the impulse is
noble, an employer-employee relationship that is squishy and
ill-defined can be problematic. And it's really where the potential for exploitation resides.

A colleague of mine, Leslie, tells me about hiring Patricia
ten years ago. "She came in with this air of formality," she
remembers. "And the first day she said, 'I'd like you to buy
me a uniform.' So I said, 'Okay, I'll buy you a uniform.'"
Leslie was mystified, but not willing to cause friction so early
in the game by denying Patricia something she felt she
needed.

After a couple of days on the job in a decidedly casual,
easygoing household, Patricia came to Leslie and said, "This
isn't really the way I thought this job was gonna be; I don't really need a uniform." "And I said, 'No, you really don't.' So
that was the end of that."

Leslie ponders that for a moment. "But she always calls me

Mrs. Shea," she says. "A lot of the babysitters before her called me Leslie, and it never worked."

If nebulousness colors and ultimately strains mother-nanny relationships in this country, it's something you tend not to find in sharply stratified class systems like England's, where nannies descend from an entrenched and largely unquestioned tradition. "Unlike with us, it's a respected profession there," says Linda, the lawyer, who lived in London for the first few years of her first son's life. "They had training, certificates, CVs. There are standards. And there's a clear protocol about what they should and shouldn't do, a demarcation between what was truly the nanny's responsibilities and what wasn't. Meaning, their work revolves around the children, not around cleaning your house or making food for you."

Linda's English nanny was of the enviable Robo variety: she made all of the baby's food herself, including meat and chicken pot pies, and pureed vegetables that she stored and froze in ice trays. "He had an incredible diet," she says.

Despite the snobbery associated with the British upper crust and its potentially toxic side effects, one frequently hears of an easy interchange, crisp and polite and altogether pre-scribed, between employer and household employee, given how culturally sanctioned and supported the whole notion of a servant class is. But here a lack of experience coupled with crippling liberal guilt can make for a very tentative boss. Stumped about how someone acquits oneself in the presence of a domestic worker, some women make the appalling choice of avoiding the problem by looking *through* the nanny, rendering her invisible—someone who doesn't have to be dealt with. "She would walk through the living room in the morning and not say anything to me, not even look at me," one nanny tells me about an awkward former boss—still hurt, if not stupefied, by the behavior. In time, pretty much all of the interacting fell to the father.

In the iffy early months, many mothers also make the mistake of not laying out their expectations, in part because they don't want to come across like taskmasters. This tendency is fueled by the subconscious hope (fantasy?) that this woman has come to help us because she *wants* to, because she *loves* us. I mean, *How could the care of my precious baby be nothing more than a way to make money?*

As a result, the mothers aren't clear and instructive about things like duties, boundaries, and benefits, about when overtime begins, what holidays the nanny can expect to have off, how many sick days she's entitled to, and whether she'll be paid for them. Again, the mothers aren't being stingy, necessarily; I think they have an aversion to all the clinical human resources–style blather that reinforces the unappealing idea that this is little more than a job.

Hence, the passionate, unbidden testimonials and little bits of proof offered up by mothers that suggest she really *does* love us. Talk to moms during the nanny honeymoon period and you will hear again and again that the nanny calls in on weekends (*when she's off the clock!*) to check on the child if he has been sick; she brings large presents in shiny foil wrap for the child on his birthday (*she always knows exactly what he wants!*); she tells the children she loves them; and even after she's done for the day and we've already taken over, she often stays a little later to chitchat with us or finish a game with the kids. Because she *likes* being here. *See what I mean? She's family!* (Never mind that in that white-glove building over on Sutton Place, she has to take the service entrance to the apartment, just like anyone else considered staff.)

They are family in only the most selective sense; given the nature of the relationship, it really couldn't be otherwise. "I knew the most intimate details of their family, the father's siblings, parents, aunts, and uncles, their best friends," says Abby, the nanny from South Carolina who worked for a family in L.A. "But nobody knew my life. It's crazy. It's not that they didn't want to, but that's what my position was, and it took me a long time to come to terms with that."

Yes, I believe Hy is like family. When our son peed in the potty for the first time late one night, we screamed, clapped, and promptly called her, not aunts or grandparents. She sounded gleeful and wholly invested in that milestone. When he had a choking spell one night and we were with him at the emergency room until morning, the sight of her moist, red-rimmed eyes and her extravagant relief as we walked in the door told me all I needed to know about her feelings for our son.

But I'll never make the mistake of thinking she's with us

for the fun of it. She has a life, something employers occasionally forget about their nannies. Early on, when there was to be a little tree-trimming party in the lobby of our building, I asked Hy if she wanted to stay late for that; it could be fun, and it was an opportunity to meet the neighbors and other babysitters working in the building. Good for her for seeking some clarity: Did I *need* her to stay? she asked. In other words, was this overtime? Because although she didn't say it in so many words, she'd rather not extend her workday an extra hour for the privilege of standing around eating cookies with some strangers on the Upper West Side. She has things to do, just like the rest of us, and would just as soon get home, thanks. Who in her right mind wouldn't, after ten hours of pouring, fetching, jostling, and wiping?

If you are lucky enough to have landed a first-rate nanny, you'll embrace this heaven-sent helper, this journeyman mom, wholeheartedly from the outset. And you'll do everything you can to make her want to stay, even when it's ill-advised, martyrish, borderline desperate, a challenge to the idea that you are in charge, and that she is doing a job for you.

"Sometimes I make my life harder so that I can make her life easier," Debra says of her nanny, Ginger. "For instance, I would never think not to give her a day off if I have a day off. Even if it's a half-day Friday, she gets a half-day Friday. My husband and I never get home late. We do everything humanly possible to get home before 6:15, because we want her to get home at a reasonable hour." (Ginger's commute is a nightmare,

ninety minutes on the subway each way.) "I make our beds before we leave; I empty the dishwasher before we leave. I
wouldn't ask her to do those things, even if I know she has the
time to, because I don't want to make her life difficult."

The way some moms describe it, there is even the inclina-
tion to impress, as if the mom is the one whose performance
will be reviewed. She imagines herself being judged by the
nanny and worries about the details that might reflect poorly
on her.

"I wonder if things are clean enough and comfortable
enough for her, because she is so perfect," Jill says. "I'm constantly removing hairs from the soap. Every night while I'm
cleaning the kitchen, I'm like, *This is Gloria's office.* God forbid
one of us forgets to take out the garbage at night. Sometimes
I have to remind my husband: 'She's taking care of our
child,'" her voice dropping to a whisper. "'Do you understand the gravity of that? She should not be inconvenienced;
there should always be money for food for her; the apartment
should be immaculate.'" Jill allows a lopsided smile, one that
tells me she's on to herself, and knows, but can't help the fact,
that this is a little bit over the top. "You know what?" she says.
"I work for *her.*"

THE WAGES OF LOVE

In truth, you don't work for her, something made plain by the
fact that she's not the one writing out a check at the end of

the week for services rendered. And yet nowhere is the potential for murk and misunderstandings, for the muddying of your role as boss, any greater than in the matter of your nanny's compensation. How can you put a price on the work she does? How can you put a price on *love*? But price it you must, because your nanny has bills to pay, too.

It's an egregiously unregulated business, where the labor is carried out in private homes that isolate employees and shield employers. The potential is infinite for unfair business practices, a lot of it admittedly unwitting. Parents themselves set the wages and ground rules based on hearsay. And no one wants to play hardball in a relationship that is ostensibly predicated on free-flowing nurture and affection. It is touching to hear, as one frequently does, that children are shocked to learn their nannies actually get *paid* for the time they spend with them. (One mother says her children were "flabbergasted" the first time they saw a check change hands.) You mean those kisses, hugs, and tickles cost money? And yet pretending this is anything but a job is to perpetuate an exploitable illusion.

According to Domestic Workers United, a group that aims to organize nannies, maids, and those who care for the elderly and establish fair labor practices, these days a decent wage for a nanny working fifty hours a week in New York City is fourteen dollars an hour, or seven hundred dollars a week (more if she's caring for multiple children). Two weeks vacation, all major holidays off, five sick days, three personal days and a cash bonus to be determined by the boss (at least a week's salary). A raise every year, typically twenty-five dollars a week. Ideally, your nanny is a documented worker, which means you will also have to pay a portion of her social security and Medicare taxes, along with her unemployment and disability insurance. Additionally, in the best of worlds, you will pay for her health insurance, or at least part of it, which can mean an extra two dollars an hour. (It is estimated that one in ten employers currently pay for their nanny's health care.) Of course, many nannies prefer being paid under the table—that is, bringing home more money each week with no taxes taken out—although that'll mean no social security payout when it's time for her to retire, and no protection if she falls seriously ill. This option is cheaper for you both in the short term, but do you really want to enable your nanny's bad long-term strategy?

No one is policing the situation. It is up to the employer to compensate the nanny fairly. In turn, the nanny must have the fortitude to challenge her employer, in lieu of a human resources department, if she thinks she's being cheated, something exceedingly difficult to summon if she's an illegal alien living in fear of being deported. Stories are rampant of power-mongering bosses who threaten their undocumented employees with reporting them.

Which isn't to say some nannies don't take advantage, too, particularly when dealing with a clueless new mother. "People were very bold about asking for a lot of money, well out of the range, but at the time I didn't know what the range was," one mother tells me about the early days. "So if you say, 'I want to pay twelve dollars an hour' and they say 'Oh no, I'm not coming for less than twenty dollars,' you're just like, 'Well, okay, I want the best—*it's my baby*! If it's expensive, it *must* be good! You lose all sense of proportion. I think people could see I was just a nervous first-time mom."

Because it is an unregulated field, nannies and employers alike keep their ears to the ground, listening for consensus, which isn't necessarily the best way to do business.

"The people upstairs gave their nanny a fifteen-hundred-dollar bonus at Christmas one year," says Zoe, a mother of two in Manhattan. "They were both lawyers; maybe the nanny worked long hours. At the time I was paying our babysitter, Joan, three hundred dollars, because I don't have her a full week"—hence, the three-hundred-dollar bonus. Miffed, Joan brought it up to her employers. "And my husband said to her, 'We don't have that kind of money to give you, and if that's what you're looking for, you're going to have to find someone else.' "

Given that Joan's job really is part-time, the three-hundred-dollar bonus would largely be considered fair in this city; Zoe is a fair and reasonable person. But the incident caught her off guard. "I think for Joan there are haves and have-nots"—whites and blacks, yuppies and immigrants. "To her, there's no continuum. And there are people in my building with a lot more money than us, people with huge apartments and full-time help that stays over. The mothers don't work; they have cars—*nice* cars—and second homes. I'm living in a two-bedroom with one of my kids sleeping in the dining room."

Zoe is the poster child for a certain kind of middle-class American: blessed by anyone's measure, educated, never hungry, loaded with options, downright rich in the eyes of most of the world, but still somehow *strapped,* essentially living paycheck to paycheck. It's the boat most of the mothers I interviewed are in, given the way raising kids taps you out on a daily basis. But to Joan, Zoe is a comfortable member of the ruling class. Surely another grand at the end of the year wouldn't hurt.

Then there are the mothers who break the bank in order to keep their nannies happy. "I live in fear of Gayle leaving me—if she only knew what I'd pay her to stay!" Janine says, half joking. "One of my friends, who'd just given birth, asked me what the going rate was these days, and I said we pay Gayle $585 a week, including her EZ Pass. And she said, 'That's funny, I talked to some other mothers who said it's more like six something.' So the next day I said, 'Gayle, you got a raise!' Because I was like, what if she starts talking to people? I bumped her up to $625.

"Two weeks later she said, 'I really appreciate you paying for my EZ Pass, but it's the gas that's killing me these days.' So now we pay $30 toward her gas. That's $655 a week."

It gets worse. "I'm supposedly on a four-day workweek and Gayle's off every Wednesday, but I never adjusted her pay to reflect that," Janine says, and shrugs. "I know it's crazy, but I don't care. I don't want her to ever be unhappy, and I feel like she deserves it."

Although nannies are universally worse off financially than their bosses, there is a funny sense in which they reflect their employers' fortunes; the attractiveness of the job and the employers offering it can sometimes be assessed in those terms. If the boss can afford perks like a car service for the nanny on late nights, chichi Christmas presents and a complimentary cell phone, it might make the job more desirable, while the no-frills boss could wind up looking second-rate and feeling insecure about the poachability of her nanny. One mother describes being utterly devastated when her employee of six years decided to leave her for a snitzy family with an ample house that had proper, comfortable quarters for her. Among the many extras: the new employers asked her what her favorite foods were so that they could stock the fridge with whatever she wanted; in addition, they had a cleaning staff, which meant the nanny's duties would be confined to the care of their baby. In some sense, the stressed, overextended mother she'd been working for just couldn't measure up. When the nanny gave her notice, the mom felt as though she'd been fired.

In cities, where vast wealth is always right around the corner, middle-class mothers can't help but feel the competition for great nannies. "Gloria's employers immediately before us were extremely wealthy, and they have this massive apartment," says Jill. "And sometimes I worry that my kitchen's not nice enough, that my chairs are threadbare." So she does what she can to make up for it, compensating with gratitude. "She takes such good care of my daughter, I feel like I should bow down and kiss her feet every day. We tell her 'I love you'; we kiss her hello. And I know it's crossing a line, but I can't help it. She *is* our family. If she's sick, we call her all weekend; if one of us is sick, she calls us all weekend."

Knowing full well that the perpetuation of our arrangement depends on our continued solvency, and knowing that we've struggled now and then, Hy's been fairly blunt on occasion about the fact that she wished we had a little more dough. I've never taken it as rude; it's just the way it is, and I appreciate her willingness to stick it out with us, a literal mom-and-pop operation that doesn't always make its numbers.

From time to time people from wealthier families will make a run at Hy, offering her a full-time job for more money. She always tells me when this happens, not by way of asking for a raise, but simply because she wants me to know. It's the right thing to do; a boss ought to be aware of these things. And she always turns them down, saying she's happy with us, because we're nice people, because we're good to her, because she enjoys the job. Generally, the conversation ends with the same wisdom from Hy: "Money is not all, Miss Lucy," she says, "money is not all."

Even though I tend to come away from these conversations feeling like a financial loser, even though she's been known to let loose with the occasional "Miss Lucy, I wish you people had money like *that*" when confronted on a playdate with Manhattan-style bounty (three thousand-plus square feet worth of unobstructed views, gleaming marble, and polished wood-work from some freshly raped rain forest), it's actually a pretty charming way of saying, "Hey, you're nothing fancy, but I like you anyway."

And that means a lot: not only would there be nice extras if we had more money, but both Hy and I know that a fancier family could offer job security—keeping her on forever, re-gardless of the children's ages and needs. Instead, my husband and I have to calculate the cost-benefit ratio of keeping her on every year, well aware that an unpleasant surprise in our fi-nancial picture could sunder this whole arrangement in an in-stant. I was taken aback one day when Hy said to me that she always prays for us—and for our jobs. Of course it makes sense; even though I know she could land another good gig elsewhere in about six minutes if for some reason we were no longer able to afford her, the situation gives the appearance of Hy's survival being tied to our employability. I just hadn't thought about her reliance on us in such stark terms.

While many a mother finds it downright queasy-making to navigate the financial dimension of this deeply personal rela-tionship, there are those who bring an almost corporate level of savvy to the negotiations, scrutinizing the home ledger the way they would the company books. Perhaps this shouldn't surprise us, given all the alpha-style career types currently in the mommy game, women who want their money's worth. But when nurture is the service being paid for, I'm not sure it's in one's best interest to sweat the pennies.

It is just a lousy fact of the arrangement that issues surrounding love and money are going to intersect again and again. For a full twenty minutes a mother I was interviewing raved to me about her nanny's many virtues—her good sense, her attention to detail, her proactiveness—describing her as the answer to her prayers. So it was a surprise when she grimly switched gears, foretelling the woman's demise, calling it unlikely that she'll be able to justify her already inflated salary indefinitely. "At a certain point, we have to stop giving her raises, to be quite honest," the mother said. "In any job category there is a threshold for how much you can make. You can't be a secretary and end up outearning your boss because you've worked there long enough. There's a certain cap to a salary title, and we're pretty much there.

"We pay our nanny a ton," she tells me, declining to specify how much. "More than anyone else on the planet." But how long she stays on "depends on how willing she is to kind of *morph*. When the kids are both in school, if she's not willing to take on more responsibilities, like shopping, then it would be difficult to justify the salary. Because it would literally burn a hole in my stomach if I were toiling away in my office downstairs and she was reading a magazine upstairs. That would kill me."

This is not what I'd call a mercenary mother—she just happens to be more realistic, and willing to speak the subtext, than most. The truth is, as the children get bigger, the job gets smaller. Even in the impossibly busy and full early years, its built-in obsolescence is the elephant in the room.

THE DAILY DANCE

I F YOUR LIFE as a mom is going according to plan, you and your nanny are now a well-oiled machine: clear in your roles, anticipating each other, making subtle accommodations as needed. The two of you communicate in a language of gestures: you leaving to-do lists, spending money and a surprise scarf or chocolates by way of thanks; her prominently displaying empty wipes containers and formula tins to indicate what staples the household needs more of, her handwashing your sweater—not her job, but a clear way of showing the love, when she's feeling it. If it's going well, your relationship is developing a graceful, rhythmic quality.

Something else has changed as well. The magical aura surrounding the woman who has come to help you out so graciously isn't fading so much as it's growing obscured by the shitstorm of everyday life. The novelty of her ministering, her powers of intuition, very quickly become necessities, something you take for granted. Where she once stood in glittering relief against the dullness and desperation of your newly over-burdened lot, she's part of the team now, up to her eyeballs in it, just like you.

Now there's less time for greetings and leisurely inquiries about her weekend. Often the nanny doesn't even have her coat off before an unhappy baby is being thrust at her. It's a mercilessly chaotic hour of the day, and moms are way past apologizing for it. The nanny has officially seen you all at your worst. I knew we were deep in our routine the morning I left for work with my daughter angry and agitated—me peeling her outstretched arms off my coat as Hy gathered her up, allowing me to make a run for the elevator. I was both distressed and relieved, all but calling out, "Good luck with that!" as the elevator doors closed on my daughter's screams.

Those motherly musts, low-grade anxiety and occasional ambivalence, can have a corrosive effect during this stage if they go unchecked. Says a mom from the New York City sub-urb of Hastings, "I had no idea how saddled with guilt I'd be by going back to work. It got easier, but it never got *easy*. And I never felt like something was going wrong; it was more just what I was missing. I was obsessed with the fact that I was go-ing to miss my daughter's first step."

It's an apt expression of the general unease that besets the newbies—although a particularly cruel brand is reserved for moms like this, who've lit out for the suburbs with the best of intentions: the desire for more space, bucolic ease, and a putatively higher quality of life for their kids is what drove them from the city. And yet thanks to the commute, they frequently won't lay eyes on them until well after 7 p.m., increasing the odds that they will in fact miss that first step.

All mothers figure out their own way of coping. Although there are myriad idiosyncratic strategies, giving up control or seizing it too tightly are two of the most common.

The Virtual Mother

Upon heading back to work, if you are not blessed with having adjusted seamlessly, you may attempt some version of mothering from afar, exerting your influence from wherever your work takes you. Your nanny will, of course, be expected to have her cell phone close at hand at all times. And you will call frequently, asking to have a word or a gurgle with the nubbin, from which you'll attempt to discern his or her level of happiness. And yes, four or five times out of ten, you will find said nubbin sullen or in tears, and it will take everything you've got not to blame it on the nanny.

Some mothers attempt to involve themselves in the daily routine by instructing the babysitter to keep a log of everything that enters and leaves the baby's body in the course of a day. On the back end that means amount, consistency, and in some cases, color and shape. The time of day all this happens is to be carefully recorded, along with the baby's reaction to it. It's not inconceivable that a real purpose for this might arise; if the baby falls ill, the doctor will have one hell of a detailed history to ponder.

But it also gives moms a comforting illusion of minute-by-minute involvement. Says Mary, the working mother of two boys in Manhattan, "How horrible is it to go to the pediatrician and have him ask you, 'On average, how many poops a day?' And you have to say, 'I don't know! Saturday and Sunday I could tell you, but during the week?'" She shakes her head, remembering the near breakdown she had when that happened to her, before the babysitter started looping her in.

Yet I would argue that there's a limit to the utility of these exercises, which can leave the caregiver feeling overmonitored and undermined. One told me about a weekend job in which she and another sitter looked after three small children. "We had to write down everything," she says, "everything they ate, what time they ate it, what time we put them down, what time they went to sleep, what time they woke up, what time we went to the park, what time we came in, how full the bottle was, how much was in the fridge. I knew I couldn't work like this. It's hard, and it's crazy."

As difficult as it can be to get there, a measure of peace is attained when you accept that your influence at home will be limited. By all means, do what you can; going out the door, do remind the nanny about giving the child only the smallest bites of food at lunch, about CPR, 911, Ipecac, and where the fire extinguisher is stashed. In weak moments you might actually verbalize the subtext, lobbing it as you leave like a Hail

Mary pass: "Our life is in your hands," you'll say, meaning your offspring is your life. Although later you will wonder, is it fair to put that kind of pressure on anyone, especially a minimum-wage employee with a heap of problems of her own?

Wherever possible, you do what you can to enforce and ritualize your sense of involvement; for instance, forestalling the children's dinnertime long enough for you to race home from work and prepare and serve it up, Donna Reed–style (even if it's just a grilled cheese). That's been my crutch from the beginning, my hedge against creeping alienation from my children: so long as I'm providing sustenance of some sort on a daily basis, I am still unassailably The Mother. So at a certain point when my kids started having trouble getting to sleep and my husband (uncharacteristically) assumed the Captain Von Trapp "only what's best for the children" pose, he theorized that the lateness of their dinnertime was at the root of their trouble falling asleep, and that Hy should start feeding them an hour or so earlier. That is, before I arrived home from work.

It didn't go over well; I launched into a piteous defense of *my role* and *my job as mother* to these kids, which rather shocked him.

He didn't get it, and why should he? My insistence on feeding the children had much more to do with me and my efforts to secure my identity as a mom, albeit a late-arriving working one, than it did with them. Similar drama ensued when my husband suggested we make our lives a little easier one harried night by bringing our son's tae kwon do uniform to the dry cleaner to have the resident tailor sew on the circular badge required by the school. *Are you mad?* I all but shrieked. *I'm his mother. I'll sew on the badge!*—despite my being comically inept as a seamstress.

By contrast, most nannies get this all too well. They understand that their doing a job so professionally and efficiently as to render the mother useless really isn't in anyone's best interest, tempting though it may be to ice out this nervous bystander and satisfy the baby with all the totems of Mom instead—a play cell phone, play keys, play compact, defunct credit card—everything but the woman herself. In the face of such potentially disruptive, high-maintenance bosses, passive aggression is not unheard of on the part of the nannies.

Ginger, for instance, has a tendency to not inform Debra of the plan for the afternoon, of where the playdates might be or if a trip to the museum is in the picture, and Debra has a pretty good idea why she does this. "Because she's with my children every day and knows them very well, and maybe because I work and she's from a culture where mothers stay home with their children, maybe she sometimes thinks she knows my kids better than I do," she says, "and she feels justified in doing things her way when I'm not around. Sometimes she can be a little defensive; it's almost like, *You don't even know what's going on during the day, so why should I consult you?* Because she's so invested in my children and she's with them more than I am—fifty hours a week, and what am I, like thirty?—I feel like she feels that I don't have as much of a leg to stand on when it comes to making decisions regarding my children."

It's no surprise, then, that mothers will from time to time reassert their role and prove they are just as invested and capable a caretaker. "This is her job, and she does know more about them than me," says Janine. "And she's usually right when it comes to strategies for making them eat better. In two years Olivia never once took a spoonful of yogurt from me, but she opens her mouth right up for Gayle." Janine offers a gentle, joke's-on-me smirk.

"Now Olivia's learning to drink from a cup. One day I gave it to her full, in front of Gayle. And she said, 'No, no, don't give it to her full; she'll spill it.' And I said, 'Okay,' but then I thought, I'm gonna give her the full cup, because that's what I would have done if Gayle weren't here. So it was sort of an assertion of power. I gave it to her and she was fine, she drank it. And I was like, oh, thank God," she laughs. "A victory over the nanny."

If it's a cardinal rule of parenthood to not contradict your spouse in front of the children, that rule is made to be broken with nannies. I rather doubt that at heart it's power mongering or spiteful when I disagree with Hy's direction when the kids are around, but it is something I feel fiercely at liberty to do. For instance, if it were up to her, the children wouldn't have a big beverage with their meal; she fears it fills them up, keeping them from the protein on the plate. Me? I have a perfectly reasonable terror of them choking on a chunk of something. Hence the importance of a cup of water on standby, something I've been brash about insisting Hy provide. In front of the kids.

For nannies, that's just part of the job. Generally speaking, even if they think they know better, they wouldn't dare say as much to the woman they work for, but woe to the nanny who actually does speak up. Celia, from Colombia, was caring for two young boys whose parents, a lawyer and a businessman, worked late into the night and rarely saw the children during the week. In the summer they went to the Hamptons every weekend, and Celia was expected to come along.

"One night we were driving to Long Island and the mother says to me, 'Why is the baby not even paying attention to me? He doesn't even want to kiss me or hug me anymore.'" She rolls her eyes. What's a straight shooter to do? "And I'm like . . . I just say it: 'Well, you work so much, you never spend time with him.' And she was like . . ." Celia's face becomes a mask of rage, a gargoylish facsimile of the mother's reaction.

"We stop at a gas station to pump gas into the car and use the restroom and she was like, *'How could you dare to say that? Who are you to say that to me? You don't know the burden I take inside myself to work and give the best for my children; I just want them to go to the best schools so they can have a career.'*"

An ugly scene, to be sure; who witnessing it wouldn't want

to gently suggest that little kids benefit more from playing with their parents and being read to than having their futures masterminded? But I can muster a little sympathy for this mother, who no doubt really believes she's putting her efforts where they'll yield the greatest results. "Obviously, I was only her employee and also much younger than her," Celia says, "but I was the one taking care of her children. That's when we started to clash."

In that sense their jobs are distinct: the nanny's in charge of the day-to-day, while the mom takes the long view. And when you consider the unbridled joy children feel when they see their nanny—how comfortable they are in her presence—I'm not sure it's only a question of the additional hours she ends up spending with them. Perhaps the nanny's uncanny ability to focus is a nice relief from the working mom's distractedness. Walking in the front door, she's reaching for the kid with one hand and working the Treo with the other. (In her dead-on novel *I Don't Know How She Does It,* English writer Alison Pearson aptly describes that fevered place, the inside of the multitasking working mother's head, as "the control tower at Gatwick.")

And in those moments when she isn't distracted, the child often becomes the object of too much focus, of overcompensation and a larger agenda. The mother's unmistakably furrowed brow when her kid can't master a game or remember the words to a song or color within the lines or give her a showy kiss before disappearing into the preschool classroom—the relationship can be full of tests and assessments concerning love, achievement, and well-being that simply don't apply with the nanny. While mothers are on the hunt for the signs of success or failure in their children, for the most part nannies bring none of that baggage to the care of their charges; they don't view the ups and downs of toddlerhood as critical evidence of what lies ahead (nor have they got the Ivy League in their crosshairs). They are here to make sure the day goes well, that everyone gets home in one piece and has a little fun along the way.

"I don't play with my children nearly as much as my nanny does," one mother tells me. "She'll be sitting on the floor, climbing into small spaces; I come home and they're covered in paint. Nothing bothers her. Everything you say to her, she just laughs." In New York City you frequently see prepubescent girls nattering away happily with the older Caribbean women who have come to pick them up, the selfsame girls who give their moms so much sullen attitude on the crosstown bus. No doubt for seriously fussed-over children, it's a nice change to be cared for by someone who can manage it with a degree of detachment.

Hard to imagine unless it happens to you, but this quality in a nanny can be a great asset to the mother whose worst nightmare is visited upon her: her child falls seriously ill. Says a mom who has been there, whose daughter's neurological problems created a host of others, "When the therapist came over, I didn't have it in my heart to force Emily to do the rehab. I would burst into tears, because in the early days, it was awful for her. But because of our nanny's determination, she really got Emily going. She was very instrumental in getting her to walk again."

A nanny tells me about the aggressively ambitious high-finance parents who discovered that their son had a brain tumor. It was a horrific three-day whirlwind from diagnosis to surgery. "It was like, 'We have to deal with this; we have to *take off from work* and be with him in the hospital,'" the nanny says. "But they don't really know how to act normal with him. They were just, like, '*How are you feeling, how are you feeling?*' all the time. Meanwhile, I can pretend I don't see he doesn't have any hair, and he's fifteen pounds overweight. I can just mess around with him, like before. But his parents don't know how to do that."

WHAT SHE'S REALLY THINKING

"They *never* do that with *me*." Every mother has heard those words from the nanny at least once or twice. Here is what provokes them: Having an easy day at the office and thinking it might be a treat for one and all, the mother decides to come home a little early, maybe take them for an ice cream, play a board game, prepare a big dinner for them for once. And what should have been an afternoon idyll of stolen hours maximized and enjoyed to their fullest turns into a bloody swamp of button pushing, neediness, and hurt feelings all around. The kids, unable to modulate their response to the specialness of seeing Mom in the daylight hours, sense her desire to make them happy, and so they overplay their hands, hitting her up like a combination cash machine and clown for hire. In turn she feels used, pecked to death by their wants. Her energy flags; she falters, and so do the children—collapsing, whining, misbehaving, as the nanny looks on. And it's true, they never do that with her: she's not vulnerable to that level of manipulation; there just isn't as much at stake.

"There have been times when deep down inside I used to think that Ginger . . . not that she doesn't like me, but that she disapproves of the fact that I left my children to go to work," Debra says. "There are no bad intentions, but occasionally I'll say, 'They've been really fresh lately,' or 'They've been giving me so many problems.' And she'll say, 'Oh, they never do that with me.' On the one hand, you know children behave differently with other adults. But on the other hand, she doesn't have to say that. That could go unspoken. She drops little bombs like that a lot."

Understandably, the nanny needs Mom to know that these sorts of shenanigans are not going on during a normal day when she's away. But in hearing it, the mom feels judged. *She's* the problem, the troublemaker. The monkey wrench in the works. Everything was fine until she showed up, unannounced. But the nanny can't say this—there is so much she can't say.

For instance, she could never reveal that she's seen it all before. While you are amazed by your little one's prodigiousness on the potty, his Mondrian-like way with shape and color, your nanny knows the drill: she's experienced the miracle of first words and first steps. From her work with other families, she's seen the collages, the plaster handprints, the autumn leaves in wax paper; she can tell you to the day when the awesome "stained glass" made from construction paper and colored tissue is coming home in the folder. This may be a first for you, but she has been down this wondrous road before.

You are aware there's a lot she keeps to herself; you wonder what she would say if she could. For instance, how do you measure up in her eyes to her previous bosses? Was there a Rebecca-like mistress, the very legend of whom mocks you? You fear your nanny's disapproval.

On one of those very rare occasions when Hy had some personal business to attend to, I happily came home early to relieve her and spend some afternoon time with the children, then two and five. "Okay, kids! Let's go to the park!" (I've always been a little uncomfortable with those quintessentially *mom*ish exhortations that never sound quite natural coming from me—that make me feel body-snatched by an upbeat apron-wearer from the 1950s.)

Winding our way down the hill toward the gate, we could hear the rhythmic metal whoop of high-flying swings, of seesaws screeching in their iron fulcrums against the playground wall of sound: the giddy, high-pitched hollering, the random song of spontaneity, freedom, and joy that continues unabated for something like ten hours until dusk—when the nannies start packing up the shovels, pails, and insulated lunch bags, loading the children into their strollers, and moving like a flock in migratory fashion back up the hill to the street.

But beneath the benign, carefree surface, a strict code prevails, for the park is a subculture of hierarchies and alliances, of territories and boundaries carefully observed. In the park there are insiders and interlopers, and you can guess to which camp the working mom belongs. Listen to the animated babysitter patter die down as she attempts to find a spot on the bench.

Undaunted, I headed rather jauntily with both kids to the swings; along the way nannies and children greeted them cheerfully by name, underscoring that sense of there being a full-blown parallel universe I knew little about in which my kids lived out healthy chunks of their day. (Consider the time my daughter was strolling along between my husband and me, and one of us pointed out a building, speculating that the apartments inside must be nice. Just a tot at the time, Sophie said, "They are"—apparently she had regular playdates in one of them. Who knew?)

Back at the park, I hoisted each of the children onto a black rubber saddle-style swing. Sophie pumped on her own while I gave Owen a hearty heave-ho, pulling back and letting him go with a "wheeeee!"—perhaps for the benefit of the skeptical-looking babysitters left and right, who always take cool interest when an actual mother shows up. So yes, I overdid it, pushing too high and hard, intermittently scanning the nannies' faces for signs of approval, but instead seeing nothing but horror. I knew not why, until I looked back at my kid, who was now dangling from the swing, his head perilously close to the ground.

Here is what happened: my experience in this area was so limited—the park being Hy's realm—that I didn't even know Owen was too young for this much speed and height, and that the bucket-style swing would have suited him better. As the babysitters tsk-tsked me loudly, I gathered him up, made sure he was okay, tried to jolly away the tears, the trace of blood— and fixated on one awful thought: *What if Sophie tells Hy?*

It isn't uncommon for a contemporary mother to sometimes feel that her baby is a stranger, a gurgling, red-faced little VIP to impress and win over, someone for whom she must nervously perform. And there's some of that with the nanny as well. We want them to think we're a good person, a good mother, which is complicated by the fact that she's doing so much of the mothering, too, according to her own sense of how the job should be done.

More difficult still, sometimes we're insecure about our abilities—about the whole arrangement—and there's nothing more troublesome than an insecure boss. A mother reports: "My babysitter has been wonderful in supporting my pumping at work, but sometimes she'll see what I've brought home and sort of look disappointed, as if to say, 'That's all you could manage today?' It made me feel so guilty that I contemplated adding water to my milk. In fact, I started to do this until I thought to myself, 'Wait, who am I pumping for, my nanny or my daughter?'"

We wonder what they think of the arrangement, of the fact that we might go several nights without seeing our children, that dinner with them is hit or miss, that we're a little vague on some of the details of their lives, like who our child's best friend is this week. I remember Hy telling me that "Jimmy Crack Corn" was Sophie's favorite song when she was a year old, and how much that annoyed me. I'd never played her the song; where had she even heard it? On a CD I didn't know about? At another toddler's house? At that little kid music class that happened when I was at work?

Nannies see how much you're missing. "A lot of them say, 'Why don't the Americans have dinner with their children?'" says playwright Lisa Loomer. "They just think it's appalling that they don't sit down and have dinner together, that the nannies are eating with the kids, and the mothers and fathers eat later. And I think the definition of respect is very different. There are ways that American children speak to their mothers and nannies that are real big no-no's in Latin culture. And a lot of the nannies feel sorry for these children, because they have so many *things,* but they don't have their parents."

It's the nanny, not Mom and Dad, putting in the long hours. Increasingly, and *because* of her omnipresence and efficiency, the parents can become a shadowy force, dashing out of work to meet nanny and child at the pediatric dentist and participate in that drama, then dashing away when it's over, avoiding the slog to and fro. It's a line parents hold for as long as they can, insisting on being present for the check-ups, although as life goes on even that starts to slip. We make deals with ourselves: *I'll attend all appointments where a needle is involved / if my kid is actually sick / if my workload isn't so bad that day.*

As for me, whereas my kids used to sprawl in my lap while the dentist examined them—me equally sprawled in the bright-yellow pneumatic child-friendly chair and hugging them tight whenever they tensed with fear—I haven't been to the dentist with them in roughly two years.

Some say the better part of parenting is in the doing, in showing up; kids go to the person they know is there for them. There is only so much the well-meaning nanny can do to bring a distracted mom up to speed. "I didn't want the mother to ever miss out on things," says Abby. "There was one day the older daughter came down to my room to tell me about a boy that had asked her out, and I knew she hadn't told her mom about it. I encouraged them to tell her stuff, and sometimes I'd give the mom a heads-up and say, 'Maybe you should ask them about this or that.'"

The best course of action for this mother at the time? Ad-mit that she hired an excellent nanny, make peace with her choices if she hadn't already, and accept all the quality help she was being offered.

Until that blessed point is reached, parents will occasionally feel like ungainly acquaintances with their own kids. When my son was a tyke, he did eight weeks at a gymnastics place in the middle of the day, so the duty of ferrying him and watching him and cheering him on largely fell to Hy, while my husband and I were at work. At the end, when they mounted a "medal ceremony" replete with the Olympics anthem playing on a boom box, my husband and I cut out of work to be there. In we clomped in dark suits and hard shoes, our phones in our pockets chirping and/or vibrating, as the nannies looked upon us like out-of-towners (Hy told us where to stand and who the instructor was). The parents in the room were so out of sync with the giggly, candy-colored scene, checking the time as their respective offices beckoned; in my mind's eye, we looked less like parents than the Men in Black, doing surveillance.

At graduation from the various preschools around the city, watch the parents massing like the press corps along the aisles as their Weeble-like young'uns scuff along, Mom hoisting four hundred bucks worth of long lens to her squinted eye. Hear the lunatic click and whir of shutters (capturing the moment on film, to be savored a few years down the road, when we're all less harried). Some parents have town cars idling outside throughout the ceremony.

I don't like picturing it, being part of it; oh those dread Escherlike moments when you find yourself morphing into the thing you're so smarty-pants cynical about, that you've so long abhorred. And yet I take comfort in the fact that it could be worse. At a recent spring recital at a fancy private school on the Upper East Side of Manhattan, a hot-ticket event for the parents spending twenty-five grand a year for their kids to attend, a phalanx of Filipina nannies could be seen holding seats for their time-challenged bosses, then discreetly slipping away and to the back of the auditorium as the moms showed up at the very last minute, sliding into the seats and assuming their rightful place, front and center.

Even the healthiest of these relationships is governed by a stark imbalance of power. The nanny isn't free to react truthfully and spontaneously in a whole host of circumstances, as when her employers fight, or when their kid is beyond obnoxious. During much of the family drama she has to appear impervious. The job demands it. But who knows what she really thinks?

You value her opinion in a fundamental way, although time and again you'll feel tested. When she calls you in the middle of a particularly hairy workday and hands the phone to your toddler so he can gum the receiver and gurgle at Mommy, it's the thing that can put you over the edge. But what are you going to do—hang up on your son? Berate your nanny for arranging what should be a treat for you both? And so there you sit, utterly trapped, as your boy launches into a lengthy, circuitous rendition of the ABC song—your nanny's chuckles audible in the distant background (what, is she folding clothes *in another room?*) Your son can't hang up the phone by himself; *when, exactly, is she planning on coming back,* you have to wonder as your workday grinds to a halt and your boss cruises past your office.

The plain fact is, some nannies do disapprove of their employers. They see the ill effects of a stressful workday as the mother reaches for the remote before reaching for her child. They see how disappointed the children are when she has to stay late at work, or go out of town, plying them with airport trinkets upon her return (*Please don't be mad at me!* the just-bought Hello Kitty purse all but purrs). At the end of a good-natured interview I'd done for this book in a coffee shop with a polite, circumspect nanny, I remember being stunned as we stood on the sidewalk, preparing to go our separate ways, when suddenly she said, "I have a question for *you*: What do you think about parents who travel frequently for business and leave their children at home for a week, two weeks at a time?"

I fudged something about it being unfortunate when jobs require that and everyone doing the best they can. She shook her head, troubled that this sort of thing is common in our culture. Clearly, she disapproved. That was all she was willing to say, but I got the feeling it was the tip of the iceberg.

"Today a nanny was telling me about a little boy," says Brenda, a nanny from Barbados. "He would beg the mother, 'Mom, could you drop me off at school today? Could you? Could you take me to see the butterfly exhibit? Could we please, *please* go see the butterflies? Could you do it, please?' He begged, he cried—and she said no." Brenda's aghast in the telling. "She couldn't do it for her son."

The nannies also see how undisciplined the parenting can be when it's done in small bursts, on the phone from work, at the end of the day, on weekends. The flustered mom who comes in the door, thumbs furiously tapping out a final batch of e-mails, is in no position to administer discipline, a circumstance the children take advantage of. Things quickly grow worse as the children lob unreasonable requests, for TV, for candy, hoping the mom will say yes just to get them off her back. It infuriates her; she lashes out—she is not in control.

So she turns to the nanny for help. And she realizes in horror how similar she must be to the dizzy mothers on those bogus-looking reality shows like *Nanny 911* that exploit the fantasy of a pro on call issuing a few facile bromides that set everything right.

WHEN THE PROBLEM CHILD IS MOM

A common difficulty nannies report is the fact that parents have seriously high standards for the care of their kids, laying down a panoply of unbreakable rules that they themselves don't enforce when the nanny's not around. Granted, it's difficult; at the end of a long day of work, what could be sweeter than popping in a DVD for the kids and opening the mail and looking at the paper, uninterrupted, despite the "no TV during the week" rule? The foolproof cure for kiddie recalcitrance at dinnertime is, of course, giving in to their desires and serving up a greasy plate of chicken nuggets and French fries, washed down with a Coke—despite the "no frozen food, no fried food, no soda" policy the nanny is expected to follow. Many a mom has shrieked in disbelief upon finding a candy wrapper in her child's jacket pocket; she knows full well the nanny is the perp and she'll reprimand her for it, despite her own frequent plying of the child with lollipops, the only sure-fire way to keep him from melting down at the store/on the bus/en route to the all-important preschool interview.

Often the parents are the greatest impediments a nanny faces in trying to do her job properly. "They complain that their children are lazy," Celia tells me about the parents of the three boys she takes care of now. "They say, 'Tell them to do this,' 'Make sure they do that.' But how can I tell them to do anything when their house has a humongous amount of junk technology"—that is, video games, TV, cell phones, and so on. "I cannot fight against these machines!"

Nannies are dependent on the fitness and well-being of the people who employ them—not only so they can keep the money rolling in and provide a paycheck at the end of the week. But also because the mother's full and steady participation is what allows the nanny to do the best job she can. The problem is, working mothers are by definition harried and ab-sentee much of the time. How does a nanny get her to do her part? As one nanny mordantly put it to me, "The baby is eas-ier than the mother."

Who among us has not shot our nanny an exasperated

glance when she expressed her need for something like quarters to do the laundry, or a few extra dollars for some supplies for the baby, meaning, *What, I'm supposed to stop what I'm doing and open my bag and look for change or singles or what have you when I'm trying to get the hell out the door?*

Well yeah, I suppose so. With any luck at that moment, you get ahold of yourself and realize she's just trying to do what's been asked of her, and not hauling that load of sheets down to the basement for the fun of it.

We've had it happen where I tell Hy to do one thing with the children, and my husband, unaware of the plan, tells her to do another. He's her boss, too; she follows the most recent or emphatically expressed set of instructions. My carefully laid after-school plan ignored, I fly into a rage (not at her, exactly). Why didn't she consult me about the change? But is it Hy's mistake to assume her bosses are in sync?

When Sophie was around three, Hy told me gently one day that she really needed a pair of sandals. It was warm out, it was park time; she had to have some new shoes. Yeah, yeah, I said on countless occasions, forgetting about it the minute I left the house. As unobtrusively as she could, once or twice more, she mentioned that my daughter needed sandals. (I was too conflicted and territorial, after all, to turn over the elemental task of shopping for the kids' clothes to her). And then one day her request sunk in, and I actually made it happen: I bought a pair.

That evening I proudly withdrew the shoebox from a plastic drawstring bag. At which point Hy subtly rolled her eyes heavenward, muttering under her breath, "Thank you, Lawd." It gave me some sense of what she's up against sometimes. (When I occasionally show up with a new pair of pants or a cute skirt for my daughter that I happened to run across at a store during lunch, I find the subsequent hoots and cheers from her and Hy to be a little disconcerting.)

It's a slippery slope. When does a mom's distractedness turn to neglect? "Your employer says she's going to be home at 6:30, and then 6:30 comes and she doesn't even call," the nanny Brenda tells me over dinner at a diner in New York City. "You feed the kids, you bathe the kids, the kids are in pajamas. And you are waiting. And then at seven she calls and says, 'Oh, I'm running late, and I might be home by 8:00.' And you didn't plan for that! Some people have to go pick up their own kids from a babysitter. This is widespread."

The fact is, parents have to remind themselves constantly of the boundaries governing the arrangement; they have to treat the employee and regard the job with a nonnegotiable level of respect, and they can't change the ground rules on a whim. For instance, if the employers spring it on the nanny that they want her to join them for the season at the newly rented summer place in Fire Island or the Hamptons (white playgrounds in utter isolation that to most nannies represent the absolute depth of indentured servitude), they have to be prepared for her to say no, and pay her regardless—not just fire her, as sometimes happens. "It's extremely hard for some nannies when it comes to the summertime," says Brenda, "because they don't know if they're going to be working."

Other abuses, conscious and not, abound. Without thinking, the well-meaning mother might continually ask the nanny to put off one doctor appointment or another, because she just can't afford to give her the time, something that could compromise her health quite directly. Or suddenly the day's to-do list, "pick up diapers, wipes, formula," has "dry cleaning" and "coffee filters" added to it. Or one morning the children are jumping up and down with the news that the family is getting a dog—a big, hairy, hungry, salivating one—whose care will largely fall to the nanny, without warning or consultation. In the eyes of some employers, the job is potentially limitless. "I made it very clear to her this was an all-encompassing job," one suburban mother tells me. "She was looking after my kid, but I was going to be home two days a week, and I wanted her scrubbing my house on the days I was home. My whole thing is, she has to do everything I would do. And if I were home, I'd be scrubbing my house. I think it's kind of preposterous to hire someone to just look after the kids; there's plenty of downtime—even when they're infants."

But the hardest part might be when a nanny is asked by parents she doesn't necessarily respect to interact with the child in ways she doesn't condone. Righteous indignation isn't always an option; quitting even less so.

Celia describes a job she had babysitting two boys on

weekends in Upper Manhattan. "They had this crazy schedule," she says of the parents, who were overtaxed professionals. "One boy was two and the other was five. He took pills for hyperactivity. I slept in the baby's room. And it was very monotonous, because the parents were always going out and we had to stay in the house. I was supposed to give the older boy a pill around seven so he could go to bed around nine, and I didn't like giving it to him. Before they went out to dinner, I would ask the mother to do it, because I wasn't comfortable. But it was my responsibility."

For starters, Celia didn't really get what the pills were for. "He was a very active boy, and in my country, if you are like this kind of boy, your parents try to find space for you so you can run and play. And this was a big building; they were on a high floor and it was like a box. He had TV in his room. Who wouldn't go crazy like that? And the parents would have fights, and the boy would be crying and trying to stop it, and I would be ignoring everything with the baby in his room. I couldn't wait for Sunday evening, because it was so depressing."

Yet even in that dreary setting, bonds couldn't help but form, beautiful connections were made. "The baby was adorable; I fell in love with this baby. I was so attached to him. He would run to the elevator when I came, and he had a name he would call me . . . Beanie? Bebe . . . That's it. It was so cute. He'd be like, 'Bebe! Bebe!' And he'd be running down the hall as I came out of the elevator." She laughs at the memory.

"Since we slept in the same room, if he didn't want to go to sleep, I'd have to pretend that I went to sleep. I'd turn off the light and he'd finish his bottle and hopefully go to sleep. But there was this one evening he wouldn't. So he gets out of his bed, walks over to mine, climbs up, and lies next to me. And then he's drinking his bottle and singing to me; these things just break your heart. And he's singing to me and stroking my face, like he's putting me to sleep. After he finished his bottle, he said, 'Shh, shh.' Then he went to his bed and went to sleep. I just wanted to hug him so much, but I didn't want to break the moment. And I felt so bad for the parents for not being able to enjoy it."

FINDING A BALANCE

If I've learned anything about relationships in general and this one in particular, it's that you get out of them what you put in. Be reasonable and kind, as opposed to penny-pinching and clock-watching; be fair, and it comes back to you double. I have been vigilant from the start about what I'll ask of Hy—for instance, making sure all of my requests and instructions were baby related during the baby years. As it happened, once I'd proved myself respectful of the lines drawn, she took it upon herself to cross them, offering to pick up the paper towels, volunteering to get the dry cleaning, refusing to take overtime pay if it's been less than an hour. Passing up that money is her choice, her gift to us if she chooses to give it, and it's just a real show of sweetness and generosity when she does. (Once I tried to force money on her for the extra half hour she'd stayed when I was running late. "Shame on you, Miss Lucy," she said, brow deeply furrowed as she pushed away my hand and the bills it was holding. "Shame on you"—cutting it that finely, worrying about the details between us that much.)

The vast majority of mothers are reasonable people, and at bottom all they ask is that they can walk into the house at the end of the day to find happy, clean, well-fed children. But beyond those nonnegotiables lies a no-man's-land of subtle judgments and differences of opinion and taste that simply have to be dealt with for the relationship to work.

Back to Hy and me: when she started with us I remember going over the bath schedule with her and being shocked by her suggestion that she give Sophie a second one after the park, "just to freshen her up," as she put it. Two baths in one day seemed a little extreme to me, and I sensed her frustration when I said so. But her commitment to a certain kind of perfection would not be denied. In no time I was coming home to find a very happy baby, albeit dolled up in something starchy, appliquéd with bears or boats or balloons, depending on the day. Matching diaper cover, lace-trimmed socks, shiny Mary Janes, hair, all twenty-seven strands, painstakingly tethered by a half-dozen clips.

Now, the elements of a getup like this would never have

been purchased by me; these were the gifts that had sat in tissue, untouched, since the baby shower. But Hy found them and happily hauled them out, while my preference for Sophie was very soft, threadbare, hand-me-down sweats, paired with a holey T-shirt.

Here was a clear case of our occasionally being at cross purposes. Not only am I a fashion-disaster/slave-to-comfort, but those sweats had belonged to my nieces, and for me they had sentimental value. But they meant nothing to Hy, whose taste runs more toward the pressed, spotless, and new. To a significant degree, Sophie's appearance was a reflection of the job she was doing; thus, sharp and tidy became the theme (to say nothing of feminine, another area in which Hy excelled and I was negligent).

So the question became: how should I handle this aesthetic impasse? Obviously, the right thing was to let Hy do her job, as there was nothing injurious or offensive or even wrong about the way she was doing it. And so it is with real shame and regret that I admit to coming home a time or two to find Sophie so kitted out in frills and bows like some pint-sized version of a Georgia Tech cheerleader that I couldn't bear it and actually changed her into sweats while Hy stood by, not saying a word. Were her feelings hurt? No doubt. Was anything gained? What could possibly be worth hurting her feelings when she was simply doing what she'd been hired to do? Would that I could have channeled a mother friend who has a nanny she loves, who once told me, "There are some days I don't like the way my daughter's hair is done, or I don't like the outfit . . . Who the fuck cares?"

(The problem, it turns out, isn't unique to me, although I do think there are degrees: said Dorinda Elliott in *Vogue* magazine in 2003, "I chafed at the way Lena and her sister and partner in nannying, Katya, dressed my boys in cheesy Mickey Mouse shirts instead of the classic Marimekko stripes I had bought in Helsinki." *The horror!*)

Most of the time my better self prevails, I hope. Some mornings Hy would show up with a greasy breakfast sandwich from a fast-food place up the street. And it quickly became a bonding ritual between her and our daughter for them to share it. Not our choice of breakfast food for her, but neither was it laced with arsenic. I let it go, time after time, appreciating the fun they both seemed to get out of trading bites, breaking trans-fats-saturated bread together.

And yet some friction is inevitable, because there will be many occasions when you are not on the same page. A friend tells me of a nanny who was sitting for them one Saturday night and reported with pride when they came home that she'd managed to get the baby to sleep without a long, drawn-out rocking and singing ritual; she'd simply calmed the child by putting him down with music and a bottle in his crib. It worked for her, reducing a typically labor-intensive *job*—let's face it—to a swiftly executed task, whereas for the mother, that rocking, singing, cooing routine is the bedrock of the relationship, camcorder fodder, something drawn out and reveled in. In this case, although it may not have made a fundamental or lasting impact on the baby, the aims, the MOs, of the two primary caretakers could not have been more at odds.

Something as mundane as room tidying can reveal the same subtle conflicts. While mothers try to collect like-minded Legos in one bin so that the tank or castle can be built and completed, while gathering all the Bionicle bits in a separate bin, a nanny might throw the plastic pieces in any old container with a lid so that the place looks *neat,* above all, when Mom and Dad return; never mind that the mishmash has rendered all the parts useless, a surefire recipe for frustration and pouting the following weekend.

But "child care" is a wildly multivalent enterprise, and room tidying is the very least of it. The critical developmental areas of potty training and sleep are where a mother and a nanny can really find themselves at loggerheads, particularly if they come from distinctly different cultures. Ellen says her nanny raised her eyebrows when she chose to "Ferberize" her son; that is, to follow the advice of the messianic Dr. Richard Ferber, brains behind the controversial method in which parents simply let the baby cry it out in the crib rather than rushing to pick him up and cajole him back to sleep. Typically, nannies from the Caribbean, the Philippines, and Latin America don't keep their shelves stocked with baby-care books penned by analytical graybeards. "I know our nanny was horrified to witness it," Ellen says of the times she simply let her son shriek. "And I remember feeling a bit self-conscious, secretly wondering if she was going to call social services on us or whatever. For the record, it worked; we got the little bugger to take regular naps."

"The potty training was a disaster, and we're still feeling the repercussions," says Maggie, the mother of twins in Houston. "I came from the T. Berry Brazelton school, where you have a 'They'll do it when they're ready' kind of mantra. But Hispanic women, especially those from Mexico, are kind of into that whole idea that swept the country about a year ago that you can train an infant to pee on the potty, that you could recognize the signs that he has to go. So she's working with the twins all day, and she was insistent that they sit on the potty. But when I got home from work, I just blew it off—I didn't want to go deal with that. So I had these three-and-a-half-year-old twins who still were not potty trained when it was time to go to preschool, and so they couldn't go. The school wouldn't allow it." Maggie heaves a sigh, convinced that the mixed messages they received confused them, possibly for life. "My son finally woke up and smelled the coffee, but we still had a lot of issues surrounding the bathroom. My daughter to this day, if she's not in the mood, just wets her pants." The twins are now eight.

It can be a great blessing when the cool, less compromised nanny takes the lead on developmental issues. A week or so before we were going on vacation, Hy made the executive decision that it was time for two-year-old Sophie to be done with bottles and bappies (the family word for that dread front-tooth splayer, the pacifier). We had talked about weaning her off these vestiges of babyhood, but hadn't quite mustered the focus or the energy. But Hy, God bless her, didn't want us hassling with that paraphernalia while we were away. And I love the image I have of her coming through the living room one day with a crumpled-up paper bag in her hand, heading for a closet, telling me sternly, "They're all in here, but we have to tell Sophie they're gone. And that's it."

The approach seemed a little extreme to me, but what the heck? I didn't have a better plan. And, of course, it worked like a charm. Sophie was befuddled and chagrinned by her bappie's absence for about a minute.

You cannot put a price on help like this. And yet the need to be boss-mom, the one calling the shots, will rear up again and again. Fussing with and redoing my daughter's outfit is so unlike me. Looking back, I wonder if that plainly rude gesture wasn't yet another mad grab for the control I'd given up the day I hired Hy—a subconscious, obnoxious demonstration of the fact that I can, at any turn, veto her decisions if I so choose. It doesn't happen often, but when it does, the unbidden force with which the pulling of rank occurs feels inspired by something primordially *mom*ish: the need to reaffirm that blood bond, that sense, however iffy, of my primacy in the household.

When I'm in the apartment hunting down a pair of shorts or a backpack that hasn't been returned to its usual spot, I surprise myself with the gut-level anger that bubbles up. It comes with knowing Hy's been cleaning and tidying and has probably found a much wiser place for those things; perhaps she's even decided to throw the shorts in the wash. And in that moment I know my annoyance isn't about the shorts; it's about feeling I've lost control of my domain.

In those odd, weak moments you'd do well to get a grip. Equilibrium in the relationship requires a lot of trust and respect, along with a willingness to look the other way from time to time. Hard though that may be. Our first experience along these lines came when Hy splashed bleach into the washing machine and discolored a load of clothes: socks of mine, sweatpants, some of the kids' nicer shirts. Hy was mortified, apologetic. We let it go—laughed it off, even—called it Hy-dying. Given the impeccable care she takes of our kids, what are a few ruined items of clothing? It simply wasn't worth it to turn it into an issue. (My husband and I both well knew if this was the worst thing Hy ever did, we were the luckiest parents alive.)

As in any relationship, this one asks that you make regular accommodations and adjustments. "There are things she does that I disagree with," says Diane, mother of two. "I don't want them getting crazy about things like being dirty, but sometimes my son will say, 'Mommy, my hand's dirty' "—a phobia he's clearly picked up from the babysitter. "Sometimes when my daughter is trying to go to sleep, I'll just let her cry for a while"—not quite Ferberizing; just making a conscious decision not to hover. "And Jen will come in and say, 'But she's just a baby; you shouldn't let her cry.' And I'll say, 'I know, I know; but the monitor is on, I'm just gonna let her cry a little longer.' And she'll say, 'Do you want me to go in there?' And I'll say, 'If you want to' "—surrendering in that moment to the caregiver's need to give care. Sometimes it's the only way.

Because just like you, your nanny has an ego, and her importance to the operation has to be underscored, continually. "After my daughter's bath, Jen will go, 'Do you want to pick out an outfit, or should I?' And I'll say, 'No, go ahead!' It makes her feel good, and it makes her feel a part of it, and like we're the team. And we *are* the team. Because my husband"—an overworked corporate executive—"isn't around. There are a lot of things that I'd be really opinionated about with other people, but it's just not beneficial for me to be that way with her. I want her to feel like she's running the show, even though she knows *I'm* running the show."

As for my colleague Leslie and her ten-year relationship with Patricia, there must have been countless snafus and disagreements. I ask her how she has managed. "Are there lots of things Patricia doesn't do well?" says Leslie, wise, imperturbable, remarkably well suited to the working-mother juggle. "I guess; she still puts the kids' clothes in the wrong drawers. I get my kids' jeans in my drawers. But that doesn't matter to me, and I don't even tell her. If I tell her, she'll feel like I don't trust her, and it's just not worth it to me." Because the part of the job Patricia does well, the important part, she does very well.

Leslie pauses.

"The one thing that's a little odd is that Patricia is very affectionate with my kids," she says. "They hug her every night when they come home from school and when she leaves. But she and I have never hugged. She'll go away for Christmas for two weeks and she'll give the kids hugs hello and good-bye, but with my husband and me she's very formal. Now I'm at the point where I don't want to hug her, because I think it makes her uncomfortable. And she'll never be in a photograph, either. We're always taking pictures of the kids, and she won't be in them. She's very shy"—despite ten years of intimacy.

So Near Yet So Far

Underneath all the demands and gestures and services rendered, the careful interactions, where do the two of you really stand? What, in the end, are you to each other? That question is likely to remain unanswered.

Debra was surprised—and, I could tell, a little hurt—to find out after all these years that Ginger has a boyfriend. She never knew. Ginger knows everything about Debra's family, from the brand of toilet tissue they buy to what the girls have scary dreams about. Why hasn't the fact that she has a boyfriend ever come up?

Every Monday morning for nine years now I've asked Hy how her weekend was, and easily 98 percent of the time she's answered me with one word: "Quiet." I wouldn't consider prying.

Proud, stoical, private, Hy is not the sort to serve up her business for my or anyone else's delectation. She's told me some things about her family; she has a grown daughter in Jamaica whose wedding she wasn't able to attend because she didn't have a green card yet (if Hy left the country under those circumstances, she might not have been able to reenter). So instead she spent nearly a thousand dollars for a deluxe, beaded wedding dress and sent it to her daughter, along with gloves, stockings, a veil, being the best mother she could be from afar.

Other anecdotes bubble up if, say, something in the news prompts her to share, as when a local crime story reminded her of the day many years before when she'd almost been killed by an intruder with a knife, the crack-crazed husband of someone she knew, looking for money. She tells me she fought him off; I can fully imagine how fiercely and how well. But for the most part she keeps her own counsel. And I'll never know for sure what sort of mother she judges me to be.

Hy actually did let me in once, a little bit. A few years into her most recent marriage, her husband grew seriously ill. There were complications involving the hospital and health insurance; I made some calls and tried to untangle a few things for her, gave her the time off she needed to take him to dialysis. I did everything I could to help, contacting a friend who works at an organ transplant unit, a legal aid lawyer who might be able to help with insurance issues unique to some immigrants. But it was too little too late; her husband was al-most gone.

A few days after he died, Hy had a number of people over to her apartment. Despite her insisting it wasn't necessary, I went, too. I'll never forgive myself for missing her swearing-in cere-mony when she became an American citizen some years back, overwhelmed as I was with the arrival of my second kid, and I had vowed never to let her down like that again. So I took the subway deep into Brooklyn from Manhattan after work with a few nanny friends of hers who work in the neighborhood.

Hy had been with us eight years, straightening, cleaning, organizing our home, dealing with our crap, and yet this was the first time I'd ever been in her apartment. It was comfort-able and tidy, in the way our home is after she's given it a good working over. There was an aquarium in the living room full of tropical fish the size of hot water bottles—for her, a vivid reminder of home, and a not uncommon household item among Caribbean immigrants. (During a patch of record-breaking cold in New York, in which people in neighborhoods like hers often suffer with insufficient heat and inattentive su-pers, a friend of Hy's had fish that actually froze to death when her heat went out. Adapting from one culture and climate to another can be difficult all around.)

There were steam trays full of curried goat and other Jamaican delicacies from a local place. There were cans of soda, some beer. And on the shelf, pictures of my kids in frames, toothy and not, throughout the years.

Maybe twenty people—a number of them babysitters I knew—sat around the living room, which was anchored by a large TV. I was the only white person there, and I could feel the culture clash; everyone was unnecessarily accommodating, offering me chairs and to get me plates of food. But I was happy to be there for Hy, who seemed so different to me in this setting. Barefoot, for one, sad but peaceful at the end of this emotionally exhausting week. Somehow she seemed less armored, either because she was thoroughly drained, or because she is always a different person at her home: not on duty, not braced for the relentless demands. As much as I've tried to make her job a comfortable, enjoyable one, I'll never really know what it takes out of her. I do know how visibly, palpably grateful she is for an unexpected day off, when I can give her one.

Hy has gone home to Jamaica several times since she's been with us; she still has a lot of family there. And every time she returns she shares an envelope of photographs she took during the trip. How I scrutinize each one—we all do, looking for the telling details of her life: her grandchildren, her daughter, her mother, her twin (how mind-blowing for all of us that there is another Hy out there), the sun-bleached stucco, the flora, the turquoise surf. Most of all we scrutinize Hy, holding babies, arm-in-arm with family. Is that her *real* home? Is she happier in Jamaica? It is shocking to think how different everything would have been for her had she stayed. But even there, the smile is that of a sphinx.

WHAT LIES BENEATH

IT IS A thing of unfathomable beauty, a child bringing strangers together, their shared love for that child bonding them for life. I have seen heat-seeking professionals transformed by nannies, so grateful are they for the grace and good care they've brought to their families. They board planes to attend their weddings, find doctors for their ailing parents, sponsor them for green cards, help them become American citizens, and send the gift of fat checks long after the nanny has left their employ.

But to get to that point, tensions of a deep sort will have to be overcome. Tensions that are simply endemic to the relationship.

CLASS

All the good intentions and genuine feelings in the world cannot disguise the fact that nannies and employers have been dealt such wildly different hands. Friction can exist in a household where the family has vastly more disposable income than the help, where they meet each other across a gaping class divide. It's almost too much to ask of someone who might live in subsidized housing, who may lack health insurance, who sends a chunk of every check back home to needy relatives, to register neither envy nor disgust in the face of the sickening plenty her employers enjoy. For nannies, it's simply part of the job to be laundering a seventy-five-dollar party dress for a baby; bringing a five-year-old to karate classes he frequently blows off that cost more than one thousand dollars a semester; cleaning up the empty, heedlessly consumed and casually discarded thirty-dollar bottles of wine and soiled linen napkins left over from a dinner party the night before that cost hundreds of dollars to throw. It is prominent in her job description to hold her tongue about it all.

In cities, of course, what the "haves" have can be jaw-dropping. Sarah, who'd done plenty of babysitting while growing up in the Midwest, knew she was in a different league entirely when she went to interview for a nanny position in Manhattan at the mother's place of business—in the boardroom of a Wall Street securities firm. The mother had a stack of resumes in front of her at the long conference table at which they both sat—"for a babysitting job!" Sarah says, still stunned, despite the fact that she's now worked for this woman for five years.

"They have three homes; they have a lot of cars, and the

kids know how much they cost. They'll say, 'Hey, the Lexus SUV costs forty-five thousand dollars, but that's not as expensive as Dad's car, which is seventy-eight thousand dollars.' They know they're rich and they think everyone else is poor." The boys are seven and nine years old.

"Their apartment is so big, the kids don't know if the parents are home," Sarah continues. "There is no interaction. The parents' secretaries e-mail *me* for Christmas present ideas, because the parents don't know. They're so impersonal with them, especially the father. He'll say, 'How was school today?'—and he won't even listen to their answer. 'Did you get your allowance? You're a good boy; here's some money.' And I'll be, like, 'Actually, he *wasn't* a good boy today,' and he'll say, 'Oh well, he's just been having a hard time,' and make excuses. It's like he doesn't even know them."

Yet even with families of lesser means, the money, the materialism, is a real issue for the women whose job it is to manage its impact, who can't afford any of it themselves. "Let me tell you something," Celia says over a coffee in a doughnut place in Upper Manhattan. "I come from a society and a country where I didn't have anything until I was twenty-one years old, and anything I have I bought myself with the money I made working. Now I see children who are ten years old and they already own a laptop, an iPod, a cell phone. Why at ten years old do you have an iPod? Why do you need a laptop? A TV in your room? I don't understand.

"Then I see three iPods on the floor two months after they

got them. I don't have the money for an iPod myself, and these children already have it. That is ridiculous. That's one thing I'm so against in American family culture"—meaning the emphasis on *stuff*. "Where are we going with all of this?"

Oddly enough, this particular family wouldn't even rank among the greatest offenders. As Celia describes it, they have a social conscience, their heart is in the right place. "These children I'm working with are interested in where I'm from, and I love to have conversations with them," she says. "They want to know about the history, about wars in Latin America, the political problems; they think Che Guevara and anarchy are cool; they have T-shirts. They are hip children. And their parents are liberals who are very aware. But the parents are the ones who gave them the iPod, the best guitar, the best this, the best that. So it's a paradox, a contradiction. They have all these books around, they have the information, but bottom line, they still carry this way of life. And it seems to me if you are in this country, you can't really get out of it."

If materialism makes the disciplining of American children an impossible chore, so does a mouthy sense of entitlement that comes with being overindulged. For the most part, they talk back to their elders in ways that would be met with a slap across the face in many Caribbean families. May, from Barbados, describes caring for two young boys in suburban New Jersey who weren't supposed to go off in the woods, and when she told them as much, the older one said, "Why don't you go back home?"

What could May say to that? She made do with this: "Well, because you didn't hire me. Your mom is the one that hired me, and she would have to be the one to tell me to go. But right now she doesn't want you in the woods."

Well-meaning parents, meanwhile, try to erase the unbreachable gulf of race and class, whether it's by small talk or forcing a glass of something on the nanny at the end of an especially hard week. "I want her to feel like part of the family, not just someone we hand a check to at the end of the week, which is ridiculous, I know," Janine from Westchester tells me about Gayle. "At the end of the day I'm her boss, and it would be impossible for her to talk to me like a sister or a mother. But I like to have my fantasies."

She tells me about the time she had an amnio with her second baby. "My husband took me home," Janine says. "We went into the living room to eat lunch. I was lying on the couch. And Gayle was eating lunch, too, but she was in the kitchen. And my husband was like, 'Gayle, come in here and have lunch with us.' And she was like, 'Oh, no, you two talk.' And it upset him. He thought that was so awful, like she was in the servants' quarters.

"One time he joked about how maybe her son, whom we've met, and our daughter will get married someday, and Gayle said, 'Awww, you wouldn't want the color.'" Janine looks crushed in the telling. "It's so obvious to me that that line is always going to be there"—the genuineness of their closeness almost impossible to gauge. "She tells me, 'I would never leave you; you guys are like my family—you treat me so well, you appreciate me'—which is like music to my ears, but I don't know if I believe her."

Despite the best of intentions, any family that's well-off enough to have a full-time nanny is likely to have a bourgeois streak they can't fight. My own family sweats the bills every month, and, still, built into the budget are the occasional pricey dinners and weekends away, and I'm never entirely comfortable with Hy's strenuous efforts to get us organized and packed and out the door on a Friday afternoon, with the snacks and the sunblock and the swim vests and bathing suits and bats and balls and all the other artifacts of a carefree few days in a rural idyll far from home. As the car pulls away from the curb and we beep, wave, and blow kisses to Hy, leaving her to trudge up to the subway and head home for a steamy weekend in Brooklyn, it somehow feels like we're asking a lot of her to do all of that cheerfully.

Of course we bring her back a gift from wherever we go— although she did tell us once, early on, when we were appallingly new to all of this, no T-shirts, please. In time I figured out why: I imagined she has a drawer full of tops from previous employers emblazoned with cute sayings from the world's fanciest playgrounds—like St. Barts, the Hamptons, and Paris, to say nothing of Martha's Vineyard, with its damned black dog mascot—that mock the fact that she'll never see these places for herself, unless paid by some family to accompany them there. The last thing she needs is another one of those. Someone really ought to print up a shirt, to be sold in tourist meccas everywhere, that says something along the lines of: *I cleaned, fed, protected, loved, and practically raised your kids, and all I got was this lousy T-shirt.*

TRUST

Rosario came into Beth's life when Jeremy was a newborn. She didn't speak English very well, but Beth and her husband could understand her. When I asked her where Rosario was from, Beth hesitated. She wasn't sure, although she thought it might be Puerto Rico. Her uncertainty is a measure of the haphazard way the child-care arrangements were made; Rosario was recommended by the wife of the building's super, and Beth was embarrassed with me about that.

She went back to work in a fashionable job at a big magazine, and Rosario took over at home. Early on, there were telltale signs that something was off. For instance, Rosario never brought Jeremy back from the park or wherever until Beth was already home at the end of the day. But she figured everything was fine, because her baby seemed happy. Beth's coif bounced as she shook her head in disbelief, telling me, "I didn't know *what* I was doing."

Things went along in this manner for a couple of months. At first Beth called home regularly to check in, but foolishly stopped doing that. A trip to L.A. interrupted the routine, and Beth got out of the habit. But no matter—everything was fine! Or so it seemed. People at her office started to say to her, "Why aren't you checking in?" So she called one day at about eleven and, true to form, Rosario wasn't home.

That night Beth asked her about it. Rosario said she had been at the park with the baby. And yet every time Beth called, she couldn't get through. In a panic, Beth called Rosario's cousin, the super's wife—the one who'd gotten her the job in the first place—who told her that Rosario took Jeremy to the borough of Queens every day so that her mother could care for him, because Rosario has a bad back. "I thought you knew," she said.

And then Beth realized how little control she'd ever had over the care of her son, ostensibly her highest priority. Suddenly it occurred to her that she didn't know where Rosario lived. She was mortified to admit it, but she didn't even know Rosario's last name. The baby was returned; the nanny was fired. But Beth will never be the same. "It seemed like everything was going so beautifully," she says.

Was Beth naïve, distracted, in denial, or just far too trusting? When I tell Hy the Rosario story, she doesn't flinch. "Oh, that happens all the time," she says, adding that there is a nanny or two in her acquaintance who've thought nothing of bundling up their charge and taking them a subway ride away for the day if they have errands or shopping to do, the moms none the wiser.

For the relationship to work, you need to trust your nanny implicitly, once you've checked everything from her references to your gut. While blind trust is foolish, earned trust is a marvelous thing—the kind Leia felt when she got a call from the cops, saying they had her toddler and nanny at the station house. Apparently a passerby witnessed her son having a tantrum in his stroller and assumed the dark-skinned woman behind him had caused it. Leia's desperate embrace of both nanny and son at the station house said it all: she knew her son was tantrum-prone; she knew her nanny was an impeccable caregiver. Indeed, the police had to admit, before sending everyone home, that the man who'd called them was a known crank in the neighborhood—a deeply unreliable witness. But Leia, disgusted by the whole affair, didn't need to hear that from them.

If you trust your nanny it's important that she knows it in her bones, for it's trust that enables her to do her job. In many ways, it's the glue. Leslie tells a story: "One time Patricia made a plan for my middle son after school. I usually make all the plans, and when I came home and he wasn't there, I said to her, 'What's the arrangement as far as him getting picked up, at what time?' And she didn't know." Uncharacteristically, she couldn't remember, or hadn't quite ironed out that part of the plan yet. "And I said, 'Patricia, there needs to be a little better follow-through.'

"Well. She gets her back up. She leaves for the night, then calls me and says, 'I can't work for you anymore. Obviously you don't trust me'—this after eight years. And then I end up apologizing, saying, 'Patricia, this is not a big deal. I have to be able to tell you things, just the way my boss at work can tell me when he's disappointed in me. And she says, 'Well, I don't think I can work for you anymore.'

"That night when I said, 'Oh my God, Patricia doesn't want to come back,' my middle son, who is very quiet and very shy and doesn't express his emotions, said, 'Mom, I don't care what you do, but you've gotta get her back.' So I basically got down on my hands and knees and I begged her."

Over time they've worked it out. Leslie and Patricia are careful with each other—"Now I'm totally gun-shy," Leslie says, although Patricia well knows what lines not to cross, too. "Patricia would never second-guess what I do. She defers, and she knows I'm the mother. I don't want to be challenged, and she's very respectful that way."

It's in the realm of trust that some mother-sitter relations most resemble a marriage. In precisely the same way you'd hoped your romantic yearnings and anxieties would vanish the day you wed, you'd like to think your concerns about child care dwindle down to nothing the moment you make that hire. In truth, the relationship is a living, breathing, organic thing that needs to be monitored and fed constantly—just like, yes, a marriage. If your nanny seems to be growing remote, it's in your interest to arrange some face time, or better yet a little gift, a token of your gratitude. If your requests are being met with muttering when you're not quite out of earshot, you have to get to the root of it. We've been together almost nine years, and yet Hy still seems to need to screw up her courage a little, drawing a breath, speaking in an oddly stiff, declamatory way when she has an issue to discuss (concerning vacation, say, or when she can have off for a doctor appointment). Which amazes me, given what a softie I imagine myself to be—although I'm sure she sees me in an entirely different way. (When she has introduced me to friends in the park, she does so formally, respectfully, with, I like to think, a hint of pride: I'm the company she works for, and there's import and meaning in that.)

Even two and three years into the relationship, some mothers find themselves second-guessing their spouselike partner. "When I was on maternity leave, Gayle took my older daughter to the playground, so I decided to go on a walk with the baby," Janine tells me. "And it just so happened that my walk went by the playground. And as I was coming up the hill my heart started beating, because I didn't know what I would find. I just said, 'Please let her be watching her and everything be okay.' So I came over the hill, where there's a great view of the playground. And I saw Gayle and my daughter holding hands and walking around the perimeter. It was really sweet"— confirmation, for now, that her trust in Gayle is well placed. "The best day of my life."

The question of trust extends to the fact that this woman works in your home and has potentially unlimited access to your stuff. If you leave bills or personal letters lying around, is she wrong to cast a glance? I'd argue not. It's hard to resist reading your own boss's correspondence upside down when it's left out on his desk and you happen to be standing there; why should your nanny be held to a higher standard than the one to which you hold yourself?

In trusting your nanny, are you counting on her to never share stories about you behind your back, to be as smiling and accepting on the subject of your family as she always seems to be in your home? Just as you blow off steam with friends by analyzing and critiquing the boss's moves to a fare-thee-well over lunch, your nanny is likely, and reasonably, doing the same with her colleagues in the park, as much as it might irk you to picture that.

The Nanny Cam Diaries

Maybe it's inevitable that sooner or later every mother is going to wonder if this woman she's placed such trust in is really who she imagines her to be. If the marriage analogy is to be carried through to it's worst-case conclusion, there are fears to face: doesn't the question of whether your mate is fulfilling his part of the bargain creep in at least once or twice over the course of your union? More to the point, what do you do about it? Does the suspicious wife go so far as to hire a detective? And is the wary mother justified in investing in a nanny cam?

Mothers have wildly divergent reactions to the whole idea. Some think of it as an intrusive, Big-Brother-like, civil rights violation, while others see it as indispensable, another set of eyes and ears. Still others fear the cam's power. "If I leave in the morning and realize I forgot something and have to go back, I always call Gayle and say I'm coming back, because I'm afraid of what I might find when I walk in," says Janine. "The nanny cam holds no appeal for me. I don't want to know."

I'm with her, pretty much. My position from the beginning has been that if I am so suspicious that I'd have to spy on Hy, then I have no business turning over the care of my kid to her. At a certain point you have to stand by your decisions. You have to walk the walk.

And yet nanny cams are a hot item, arguably another way for absent moms to insert themselves into the domestic sphere from wherever they are. Without question, they provide a mesmerizing look at what goes on at home, capturing scenes that no mother could have imagined.

TAPE I

Debra couldn't possibly trust Ginger any more than she already did. And yet everyone was wiring their kids' rooms. She'd heard a few bad stories. Was refusing to install a camera like sticking her head in the sand? She couldn't afford to do that to her daughter. So she leased a nanny cam that masqueraded as an air freshener appropriate for a child's room, a little box that had the alphabet on it and a pinhole concealing a wide-angle camera lens.

"The day I taped Ginger was the day before my daughter's

second birthday," Debra says. "I was just beside myself with anxiety and fear, completely upset about what I might find when I watched the tape. And what we saw was that she'd brought a present, Danielle's first bicycle, and she was teaching our daughter how to ride it. Then she was reading to her and putting her down for her nap, kissing and snuggling her." Debra exhales.

"I was so relieved—it was the most incredible relief I've ever had in my life. We were told by the company who rented us the camera not to reveal that we had taped her, because then other nannies would grow wise to it. But I felt I had to—I thought it was only fair. So I told Ginger and apologized, and said she was doing an amazing job. She was very understanding."

Perhaps she was. Although what a strange thing to learn, in retrospect. Not that it makes it any easier, or the relationships any less complicated, but the twenty-first-century nanny *is* savvy about this sort of thing. While Hy was working with another family years before she came to us, the toddler in her care once piped up, "Mommy was watching a video and you were in it!" And no, she wasn't particularly shocked.

TAPE II

"I came home early one day and my son was in his high chair in the dining room, and the babysitter wasn't in there with him," Martha says. "And, I don't know, she was putting some laundry away in another room and my heart kind of clenched. So I said to her, 'You always *do* sit with him when he's eating, right?' And she said, 'Oh yes, yes, yes, I was just out of the room for one minute.' Plus, he had a dirty diaper. And when I spoke to her about that, she started crying, telling me she loved the job. She got very emotional, and I fell for it hook, line, and sinker. I said, 'You know I'm so delighted to have you; don't worry, it's just a small thing.'

"Then I had lunch with a colleague, and she told me about videotaping her nanny. A friend had done it and it was disastrous. It's not like she was burning cigarettes on the kid, but let's just say it's not the reality you imagined when you left for work. I think the nanny was in front of the TV all day. So I said, 'Well, I'm not at all concerned; my nanny is really religious and everything.' But I will say I'm a realist, and I made the decision right then and there that I was going to videotape her. She gave me the name of the agency; we got the camera and put it in my son's room in a toy, maybe a jack-in-the-box.

"So we come home and watch it one day. I totally had no anxiety. We turn it on in our bedroom, and the first thing I saw was that she was pulling down the shades in the morning. Our son doesn't take a morning nap; what's going on?

"So she's pulling down the shades and talking on the phone the whole time. Our son's in his crib trying to get up, and she sort of smacks him down—she's on the phone and she didn't want to be bothered by him. And then, when she was changing his diaper, she was being really rough with him. It was like she was flipping a pizza. Then later in the day, he's trying to play and she's just standing by the window, bored." Martha goes slack-jawed at the memory of it. "My husband and I nearly had a nervous breakdown. It was the single worst experience of my life, because it really made me feel the most trenchant human emotion you can experience: betrayal.

"What was so freakish to me was the duplicity," she says. "I believed she had been one person, but then I saw this other one. I was sobbing for days. I had assigned traits to her that frankly she hadn't evinced, and I felt sick about that. We got rid of her right away."

No, Martha didn't witness abject neglect. But you get the feeling she saw what she needed to see. In truth, she'd been less than sure about this woman from the start, however subconsciously, and streaming video of anyone's day with a baby can provide you with the narrative, the proof, you're looking for.

TAPE III

While most people who use nanny cams rent them on a temporary basis, others actually purchase their own. "We bought one because I knew I was going to be a habitual user," Kelly says with a laugh. A suburban mom with a background in investigative journalism who's done her share of undercover work in the line of duty, she had no problem whatsoever with employing surveillance tactics in the difficult task of convincing herself she had hired the right person for her children.

"I'm big into the nanny cam thing, because I feel there's no reason not to use one," she says. "I'm not embarrassed by it. I feel like it's a great tool; it's not illegal, so why not? You're protecting your most important possessions, really. And if I'm putting on an alarm when I leave the house so someone won't burglarize it, why wouldn't I want to protect us from a nanny who I'm just getting to know? And I'm really glad we did, because we were able to root out problems."

Kelly's first nanny cam experience went like this: "We hired this woman. I'd vetted her credentials. I did my own criminal background check on her, did my own driver record check. I called the families she'd worked for. I'm not shy. I asked point-blank questions: Was she responsible? What problems did she have? Were they resolved? And they thought this particular person was great. I mean, I did everything—crossed t's, dotted i's, bent over backwards—I was anal-retentive, the whole nine yards. And she passed with flying colors. So we hired her.

"Long story short, what the nanny cam reflected when my husband and I turned it on every night was not abuse. It was just that when she was sitting down for lunch, it was *her* lunchtime. My son was toddler age, holding his hands up, like, 'Pick me up, pick me up,' that kind of thing. And she wouldn't even turn towards him, wouldn't even pay him any attention, wouldn't even motion at him. She wouldn't push him away, she wouldn't do anything to harm him physically, but it was this emotional break, and that's not good, that's not good enough. I just felt like she was very attentive when we were there; she'd put on this wonderful show. But I set a pretty high bar that I wanted her to meet. When you're a mom, nine times out of ten you're gonna put your kid on your lap while you eat."

Over the next few days in Kelly's home, the nanny cam was pressed into service again, and each time it revealed the same thing: no outright abuse; just a depressing lack of doting focus. Kelly and her husband decided to fire the nanny.

"And honestly it was the easiest thing. She walked in one morning—she had barely got through my threshold—and I said, 'I don't think this is working out; I don't think you're paying enough attention to our son. And I have made the decision that today is your last day. In fact, you don't need to work today.'"

The nanny still had her coat on. And no, she wasn't told that a nanny cam had been involved. "She didn't ask," says Kelly, incredulous. "There was no surprise, no defending herself. I mean if you just got fired and you thought it was for no cause, you'd want to have a conversation. You'd want to explain yourself: 'Oh, I had a bad day,' 'I'm going through a rough patch.'

"But here's the greatest example of why I made the right decision: she didn't even say good-bye to my son. It wasn't even like there was this wonderful bond she cared about." In fairness, she'd only been with them about a month, Kelly tells me; "it wasn't long enough for her to be head-over-heels in love with him, but it's enough for her to actually be a human being and say good-bye to him."

I nodded knowingly and grunted and tsked in agreement during Kelly's tale. And yet, on reflection, I'm not at all sure I agreed that the nanny should have been playing with the child while she tried to eat her lunch. Any caregiver, be it a mom or a nanny, needs a break at some point. Is eating lunch with a baby on your lap really part of the job? Would I like it if a colleague planted herself on the desk in my office watching me while I took twenty minutes to choke down a sandwich— would that leave me feeling refreshed and ready for the second half of my shift? Is it fair to expect a nanny to never switch off the smile, the extreme focus, to pretend she is as invested as the mother?

I'd argue that nannies are entitled to a bona fide, baby-free break during the day, so long as it doesn't leave the baby in harm's way. I also wonder if there might be some sort of developmental benefit to the child's learning how to entertain himself now and then.

As for the nanny's unwillingness to talk it out serving as confirmation of her guilt, that might be Kelly applying a white-collar notion of justice and due process to someone who lacks a working knowledge of either. And it is too bad the nanny didn't say good-bye to the baby, although I think you'd have to have some rare fortitude to rebound on a dime from that brazen rejection, with it's shock value, its dire financial implications; how hard it would be to have to come back from that, to put on the happy face for a toddler you'll never see again. Yes, Kelly set a high bar, not only for the nanny's behavior on the job, but also for her comportment at the firing. She isn't surprised the nanny failed there, too. "It was vindication," Kelly says. "I was thrilled."

TAPE IV

"Six months after my first daughter was born, I had to go back to work and hire a nanny," says Terry, who works in corporate finance. "And the woman I hired, who was with us for a year and a half, was late frequently, a half hour, forty-five minutes. So my husband would yell at her. And one day she walked out, leaving a note that said, 'I will not be yelled at.' And she never came back.

"So I panicked. Then a good friend at work decided to move from Manhattan to New Jersey, and her fantastic, wonderful nanny was available. Let's call her Rita. She was from British Guyana. And she was really fantastic from the start: soft-spoken and kind, but mature, with a lot of common sense. Firm but loving, she knew how to discipline without raising her voice, ever. She was great to work with. If someone had to come to the house to fix something, she could be trusted to explain it. If she had to go to a new doctor with the children in some new neighborhood, I could just write down the address and she could be trusted to take the train and transfer to a bus and arrive on time and bring the medical form. And she befriended the other nannies, but wouldn't let them take advantage of her. She was able to manipulate that social world very well."

Terry peers at me through fashionable specs over her glass of wine. It's easy to picture her as a master of efficiency on the job, someone who doesn't suffer fools. "Rita was also very savvy about keeping me feeling connected. She would call me at work and say, 'Listen to what your baby wants to say to Mommy!' " before putting the child on the phone. "And she never overstepped. She had her own children, so I never had to worry about her getting too close to mine. It all went like clockwork.

"The day my second child was born, she came to the hospital and brought my older daughter and bonded with the baby instantly. The baby loved her, and they had a wonderful relationship. She really thought of this nanny as her second mother, and I thought of her as my partner. My husband got along with her wonderfully, too. She knew instinctively how not to make him angry. Because he's sort of a yeller, and she was very sensitive to his idiosyncracies.

"Even my daughters' teachers said, 'This is the best nanny we've ever seen.' My older daughter's kindergarten teacher said, 'When I retire and I need someone to take care of me, I'm hiring away your nanny, just so you know. We've watched her from afar with the children; she's so patient and kind.' All of my neighbors wanted my nanny. They'd come up to me in the hall and say, 'You have the best nanny we've ever seen.' I'd say, 'Yes, I know, thank you very much.' Because of that, I paid her more than anyone else in the building on purpose, because I didn't want to lose her. By the time we let her go, she was up to seven hundred dollars a week." Terry pauses, takes a sip from her glass.

"I also gave her spending money. In the beginning I'd say, 'Let me know when you use it up and I'll give you more.' And the first few months she gave me receipts. I'd kind of look at them and throw them away. Then I got lazy, and I stopped looking at the receipts. And I stopped asking for them, and she stopped giving me them. She'd kind of tell me at the end of the week what she used the money for: she took our daughter out for pizza with the other kids, they'd have to have an ice cream, she had to go to the drugstore to buy more swimming diapers, and they're expensive . . . and the amount I gave her went from twenty dollars to forty dollars to sixty dollars to eighty dollars. And I was like, well, that's what it costs. We were not at all suspicious.

"Because of my husband's business, he kept a lot of cash in the house. Also, after 9/11 we liked to have it around in case of an emergency. But he didn't keep it locked up—he kept it in a cabinet in the area of the apartment that he used as an office. And some weeks I'd say, 'I need money to pay Rita; I'm a little short.' And he'd open the cabinet, and yes, on one or two occasions he did it with her standing there. But we didn't think anything of it. She's practically part of the family.

"Eventually he noticed that money was missing. He asked

me if I took it. I said no, and he said, 'Maybe I added wrong.' The second time he noticed it, I actually had taken some. The *next* time, he said, 'Did you take money?' And when I said no, he didn't believe me.

"In November he'd gotten one hundred dollars worth of crisp, new five-dollar bills to be used for when our older daughter's teeth started falling out. And one day he came home from work and went to get a five, because our daughter had lost a tooth, and there were no more fives. He said to me, 'Did you take the tooth fairy money?' And I said, 'Are you out of your mind? How could I possibly take the tooth fairy money?' A bell sort of rang for me, but not for him. He didn't want to think about it.

"Christmas rolls around and now we have substantial cash to pay all the tips"—to the doormen, the building super, and so on. "A couple thousand dollars. And when he went back two days later after getting the money, there was a thousand dollars missing. He said, 'I think someone is taking our money. Who could it possibly be?' And I said, 'Well, one thought comes to my mind,' and he said, 'No! Not Rita. It must be the cleaning lady, or the porter.' I said, 'If this were a detective novel, it would be the nanny.'

"So I called one of those nanny cam places, but it was expensive, and I thought, should I really wire up the whole house? This seems crazy. Finally, my husband took his video camera, which has the capacity to tape for only one hour. And he laid it down on his desk aimed toward the cabinet and turned it on *Record*. There's no sound, no red light, so you wouldn't know it was recording. And he left the house.

"A few days later while I'm out with the kids at some class, he watched the tape. Then he called me on the cell phone and said, 'Get home right now.' When I got there he was crying; he'd burst into tears watching it. What he saw, within a few minutes of his leaving, was Rita very clearly walking over, opening the cabinet, taking out the envelope with the money, going through it, counting it, taking some of it and putting it in her pocket, putting the rest back, closing the door, and walking away. He almost died, he felt so shocked and betrayed.

"When I saw it, I felt like I'd been kicked in the stomach. I felt angry, hurt, miserable, devastated. It wasn't even about the money; it was about the trust. I mean, she was married, her husband had a job with benefits, and they lived in a decent house in a decent neighborhood. She had her green card. She was mature. She seemed solid, not like some nannies who you know are in a bad place financially."

Terry shakes her head. "My parents pleaded with me to keep her, 'She's such a fabulous nanny; what if you make her pay it back? What if you take it out of her salary?' And I said no, because that's where I *live*. That's where my credit cards and my checkbook and my jewelry and my things are. I can't give her access to that any longer. So I needed a couple of days to figure out how to handle it. The hardest part was acting normal with her during that time. We also didn't want the children to get upset or find out what was going on.

"Then one day I came home and said to the kids, 'Watch TV in the living room; I have to talk to Rita alone in my bedroom.' We'd ordered a safe from Staples and it had arrived that day. She seemed nervous about it; the box had a picture of a safe on it, and I had a feeling she knew. So I brought her in, closed the door, and said, 'You broke my heart. I know what you did; I have you on tape. I can't believe you would do this to me.'

"She looked serious and nervous, but she didn't deny it. She said, 'I'm sorry, I never meant to hurt you, please believe me. I was sending the money to my mother in my country because she needed it.' And I said, 'She didn't need it enough that you had to take it from me.'

"I said, 'This is what you have to do for me. You have to hug and kiss my children and say that you have to leave and not be their babysitter anymore, but it's not their fault. Number two, you have to never come anywhere near my children in the future, and if you do, I'll prosecute. Number three, you have to give back the money.' And she just quietly took it without getting upset and followed my instructions. The little one cried when she walked out the door."

As it turns out, Rita, on the face of it, was such a superior nanny, it was hard for anyone who had witnessed her in action to believe she was capable of deceit. Terry offers up a postscript that makes a lousy story just that much worse:

"I'd gotten Rita's niece, who's in her twenties, a job as a nanny of a friend of mine, and so she was working in the neighborhood. And she told my friend that she heard that I'd fired Rita because she was too close to my younger daughter, and that I was jealous. That my younger daughter was supposedly calling her 'Mommy'—which isn't true. Rita was so clever and smart that she quickly came up with this plausible explanation that other nannies would certainly believe. But even when I told my *friends* the story, I had to show some of them the tape for them to believe me. When I told a friend of mine who used Rita on the weekends, she said, 'Rita already called me and told me that you were going to tell me this crazy story, and that it wasn't true, that it was all a misunderstanding. Are you sure it's not a misunderstanding?' " Terry gapes at me, incredulous. "I mean I *knew* this woman, I'd *worked* with her! I said, 'I have her on tape.' And then she said, 'Well, she wouldn't take money from me. Maybe from *you,* but not from *me.*' Click."

The family has rebounded; now there is a new nanny on board. "She's nice, kind, and loving, but she has absolutely no common sense," Terry says, with characteristic, unflinching candor. I get the feeling the Rita debacle has drained her reservoirs of sentimentality where nannies are concerned. "I have to be very specific with her, and I have to assume she's going to screw up. If I leave a note for her to pack a change of clothes for the kids, she'll *change* their clothes and cross it off the list. So what I take from the experience is, there is no such thing as the perfect nanny. It's a tough relationship; it's a hard job. When I talk to my friends, they say, 'My nanny is loving and kind to the kids, but she has a bad attitude with me.' Or 'She's messy,' or 'She wants too much money.' I thought Rita was the only perfect nanny around, but even *she* wasn't. There is no such thing as the perfect nanny."

This idea of perfection. Is your husband perfect? Are your friends perfect? Your assistant? Your boss? Why, when it comes to nannies, should this even be upheld as a possibility? Mothers need to face the strange truth that the nannies in their lives, by virtue of the unspeakably challenging and important service they are providing, simply are expected to meet a different standard. It's understandable; a misstep could mean serious injury or worse for the child. And yet it's not a reasonable requirement. Mothers, in their role as employer—something they make up as they go along—display egregious lapses in judgment and decorum all the time; it stands to reason that nannies will slip up now and then, too.

Of course, stealing is something else entirely. That's inexcusable on any job. "I would never have let this happen to me at work," Terry says, describing herself as a skeptical, suspicious person by nature who, in the case of Rita, nonetheless actively ignored the warning signs. "I've fired several people in my office. I would so quickly figure it out and put them on warning or probation. If they're not doing the job, whether you like them or not, you fire them and get someone else who can do it. But you can't do that with a nanny, because there are so many factors. It's not a normal employer-employee relationship; you're not even with them all day. Yet you rely so heavily on this person, and you don't want to go through the pain and agony of finding a new nanny. In the back of your mind, you're always thinking, *Can I do this to my children?*" At all costs, then, you resist the urge to make a change.

What might provoke a nanny to steal or otherwise betray her employer's trust? For starters, there is the matter of need, as so many women who perform these jobs come from economically devastated circumstances. I've heard from a number of nannies who say they are looked upon from family back home as riding the gravy train because they managed to make a life in America. Despite their minimum wage status, they are thought to be wealthy, and relatives expect a share of the pie. When they go back for a visit to the Caribbean, they sweat the Santa-sized load of goodies they're expected to bring to the extended family.

Needy relatives isn't a justification for stealing, but it is a reminder of the yawning gulf that exists between the American business-class crowd and the immigrant women looking after their kids. Most of us don't know remotely what it feels like to live on the edge. We're all operating with a safety net of some kind.

But there's something else. When relationships between mothers and nannies end badly, more often than not a line has been crossed. Or the boundaries were blurry to begin with. If theft is the issue, it sometimes turns out that the employer flashed the dough, or revealed the secret stash, just as Terry's husband did with Rita. Perhaps that bespeaks a subconscious need to test the situation and come up with solid proof of the nanny's loyalty.

In July 2004 a story appeared in *New York* magazine by a woman who routinely asked her cherished nanny of four years to withdraw money from her account at the ATM "when I was low on cash and strapped for time," as she puts it. That is, she supplied the woman with her bank card and pin number, entrusted her with them. How shocked and hurt this mother was to learn, down the road, that the nanny made additional withdrawals and pocketed the money regularly, as much as sixteen hundred dollars in a single day.

The lunch, park, and preschool crowd nattered about this one for months. The nanny-free moms clucked at the inevitability of it all; many could not believe this mother's naïveté. Of course, other mothers could understand her trusting the nanny with something as private and confidential as her personal finances, given that she trusted her with her children, the most precious thing of all.

As for me, I questioned her putting the nanny in such a difficult position; that is, handing over the magic card to someone of far lesser means, who may not have a vat of cash just sitting there to be tapped when the mood strikes. Which isn't to suggest that the mother was flaunting her wealth, cruelly manipulating the less powerful person in the relationship. Rather, I suspect this well-intentioned mother was willfully oblivious to the socioeconomic issues between them. Either that or she was unknowingly administering the test she was certain her nanny would pass: Deep down she needed to feel that all that good service came from a place of love, that the nanny's role defied job description, and that she could be trusted with anything.

It's both infuriating and touching—the mom's disregard for boundaries, her Pollyanna-like misinterpretation of their arrangement. "Just because a nanny is loving toward your kids doesn't mean she loves you," she discovers. And later in the article: "I was slapped with the realization not just that a friend had suddenly become a stranger but that maybe she'd never been a friend in the first place." Maybe not.

Speaking of the salad days long before things went horribly sour with her nanny, one mother tells me, "I was happy that my husband and I could have a tiff or a disagreement in front of her and not worry that she would blab it to the neighborhood. At first we'd be a little careful around her, but then it was like, so what? She'd never embarrass us. She knows about our issues; the woman washes my underwear."

I remember a morning a year or so ago when my husband and I were trying to pull things together before a long weekend. As we started going through the tedium of what had to be accomplished in the next eight hours, the supplies that hadn't been purchased, the checks that hadn't been written, I recall us starting to snipe a bit and actually raise our voices, perhaps putting on a show for Hy, who was busily working one room away. I'll never know exactly what our problem was that day, although I guess we felt some low-grade exhilaration in Hy seeing the real us and our not having to hide or be careful with her. We liked knowing that she was there for us regardless, that she was family.

So where's the line? When does your casualness as a boss begin to taint your authority? One mother who discovered her beloved nanny had stolen money from her told me in a separate conversation that she routinely walks around her home "in my bra and my underwear right in front of " the nanny working for her now. "I'm like, you know what? If you're gonna be in my house in the morning, you're gonna have to see me in my bra and my panties. And that's it. I can't avoid it; it's my house, darn it, and I'm walking around the living room just like this. She'll have to deal with it. And of course she doesn't care, but . . ."

I'm taken aback by the unconscious ambivalence. She makes it sound like the nanny has forced her way into the situation and as such must put up with whatever she finds there. In truth, it was the mother who made the decision to bring this woman into her life's inner sanctum, and her uncertainty about that manifests in undies: there's another mother figure on the premises, with a significant amount of influence over her kids, so the real mother marks her territory with bra and panties, laying claim to the space rather flagrantly in a way the nanny never could.

She likes to think the nanny doesn't care. And yet who in the corporate world has to see her boss in boxers—or a La

Perla bra and panty set—or hear her arguing with her spouse? Letting it all hang out to that degree can have a corrosive effect. Haven't we been told since childhood that if you're intimidated by a figure of authority whom you have to face or perform for in some way, just imagine them sitting there in their underwear? That tactic is about undermining the power someone might have over you to the point of rendering them foolish. Porousness in the boundaries that define your roles is more often than not the beginning of the end.

Nanny Recourse

Given their relative wealth, savvy, and options, to say nothing of their discreet powers of surveillance, employers unequivocally have the upper hand. And yet just because a nanny tends to suck it up smilingly when the physically and emotionally taxing child-care tasks are heaped upon her, underestimating the toll it takes, as well as her stake in being compensated appropriately, is a grave mistake. True, a lot of aggrieved, oppressed nannies wouldn't know where to start in trying to find fairness and justice. But that is beginning to change.

In October 2005, I attended what was billed as a tribunal at Cooper Union in New York City, sponsored by Domestic Workers United, in which a number of nannies and babysitters approached a microphone to describe to a learned panel of human rights experts the abuse they have suffered at the hands of their employers. In essence, they were testifying and asking the like-minded panel to symbolically ratify the legitimacy of their complaints and make recommendations. The chief recommendation sought by all was for a bill of rights to be presented to state legislators that would ensure the sort of labor standards and protections enjoyed by most sectors of the workforce, domestic workers notably excluded.

"Paid domestic labor is the backbone of global cities like New York, yet domestic workers are paid next to nothing," nanny Joycelyn Campbell thundered into the microphone. "I have seen employers having *dog parties* costing more than some people's weekly wages." Hisses and hoots from the nanny-filled audience. "This is true! I've seen dogs chauffered to out-of-town groomers, while some nannies work long hours into the early morning and are not even given taxi fare." Audible disgust; knowing nods.

"We care for the most important elements of our employers' lives, but we are treated as less than human. No sick days, no vacation, paid late, no health care, fired if we get sick or pregnant. Eleven, twelve, fifteen hours per day. We are here today to put the US government and the New York state government on trial for forcing domestic workers to live and work in the shadow of slavery."

The abuse, it was pointed out, is systematic, given that the laborers work under conditions that are exceedingly difficult to regulate. Furthermore, federal workplace protections only apply to companies that employ a minimum of fifteen people. Even worse, so many women who do this job are undocumented workers ripe for the exploiting, given the catastrophic risks of making noise. Such women typically don't even know what their rights are, let alone how to safeguard them.

It was a serious gathering; you could feel the anger and sadness among the few hundred people in the auditorium. A lot of women from the Caribbean, from Central and South America, and a smattering of college-age girls with an array of piercings, haphazardly cropped hair, and notebooks.

The parade of luckless women, the litany of abuse, was horrifying and ultimately numbing. We heard from Marina, who cared for a disabled child—carrying him to the bathroom, bathing him and brushing his teeth, on top of doing the cleaning, ironing, and cooking. She slept in the basement where the sewage frequently overflowed, all for two dollars an hour. We heard from Elena from the Philippines, who worked for a prominent New York family who didn't allow the help to use their utensils. Instead, they had to use plastic, which was to be washed and reused. The lady of the house was a screamer who required the help to stand when she entered and to never look at her directly. We heard from Violet from India, whose boss once removed one of the sandals she was wearing and hit Violet in the face with it.

We heard from Tati, whose boss yelled at her "to the point where I was becoming sick with depression and nervousness. I left my last job so exhausted and destroyed I could only think of hurling myself in front of passing cars, because I was made to feel so bad, I wanted to die." We heard from Windy, who looked after three children, a dog, and the boss's brain-damaged brother; cleaned the house; and maintained the vegetable garden in the summer, all for the unlivable wage of about two hundred dollars a week, with no days off. It was the sort of job where she'd be roundly berated for putting the salad fork on the wrong side of the plate. But she had no leverage with these people, because she didn't yet have a green card.

Someone came and spoke for Cindy, who was too sick to attend herself. According to the testimonial, her employers didn't give her certain holidays off, because, they claimed, since she was not an American, the holidays were not for her. They also threatened to fire her if she didn't hurry back after a surgery, then gave her a hard time when she had follow-up doctor appointments. Things only got worse from there.

Although I couldn't imagine any of the mothers I know being at the root of this kind of abuse, these worst-case scenarios were instructive. It's a finer line than any of us might imagine between fair treatment and neglect, given how un-flappable nannies can appear.

When there were no more women to share their hardship, the panel adjourned for deliberation (their ultimately return-ing to recommend a domestic workers bill of rights was not in question). During that time, the women were led in a rousing chorus sung to the tune of "The Battle Hymn of the Repub-lic": "*We want justice and we want it right now / so listen to what we say . . .*" Fists split the air as the women whooped and jumped to their feet, chanting: "*Domestic workers united will never be defeated . . . domestic workers united will never be defeated . . .*" The room was alive, electric with defiance, these lovely looking women who minister so sweetly, now rowdy, angry, and righteous as they awaited the recommendations of the tribunal, for a just wage, time off, health care, and so on.

Watching the scene, all I could think about were those mom friends who couldn't cope a day without their nannies—each one of whom, I'm fairly certain, considers herself an ideal boss and her nanny a satisfied employee. And maybe they are. Still, how shocked they would be to see this.

TAKING STOCK

IT IS NOT overstating it to say that if we didn't work, if we didn't lean so heavily on nannies and our nonworking friends, we'd be different mothers entirely, a hypothetical that prompts ceaseless questioning and fantasizing. Often the sight of another note in the kids' backpacks, or another reminder, another plea for five dollars in an envelope, another request for chaperones for a class trip pushes me to the brink of tears; sometimes it's really just too much on top of what I'm facing at work. I've had my share of low moments as a mother prone to job-related distraction, often forgetting things like "Alphabet Day," on which your child is supposed to bring in something that begins with that day's letter. (With Owen empty-handed on G Day as we walked into the schoolyard, I thought fast: his shirt was Green and he was wearing a Gap sweatshirt—never mind how disappointed he was not to be carrying a plastic Gorilla.)

One rare day during the preschool year, I came home early

so I could take my son to school (he was in the afternoon class). And no, he wasn't being remotely facetious when he said, as we set out, "Mom, do you know where my school is?" Another time he surprised me by asking not for a Power Ranger or a Spiderman Web Blaster or a monster truck, but for a haircut. I truly had not noticed that his bangs had grown past his eyes.

But with my life being the way it is, things like haircuts will fall through the cracks. I don't think I could do it any other way. Or could I?

I consider the case of Sharon. Our daughters were in the same class in pre-K. She was an attentive, well-equipped stroller schlepper in jeans—a bit stiff-upper-lipped, I thought; she had the classically selfless stay-at-home demeanor. I was surprised to learn that she'd been a successful, driven litigator in her former life, pre-kids (that being pre-K for moms).

Occasionally, a number of the mothers from that class would indulge in that id-fueled thing known as Moms' Night Out. The blender drinks flowed, the quiet desperation growing louder by the second—our respective issues passed around and feasted upon like a platter of dim sum. One such night, Sharon was doing some loquacious reminiscing about her glory days in the courtroom when suddenly she raised herself up to her full, elegant six feet in the middle of the restaurant and treated us to a dramatic reenactment of one of her finest moments before the bench, gesticulating, recapping closing arguments, explaining her strategy. I was transfixed; it was a stunning performance. And poignant, I thought, this onetime lioness of the law profession channeling her former self, reliving her glory days with us.

Apparently, after her daughter was born, she just felt she couldn't do both. Three months into her maternity leave, she had to give an oral argument in the state appellate court. "A very simple, straightforward case," Sharon tells me, tucking her feet beneath her as she reaches for a glass of wine in her brilliantly appointed Deco-style apartment. "But it was the most difficult thing I've ever had to do, I think. Preparing it was just—all of a sudden it was just mentally beyond me. I wasn't thinking in complete sentences. I couldn't follow through. That really threw me for a while."

Eventually she left work entirely. What the transition required, Sharon says, "was a lot of tearing away of layers of myself. When you walk into a room and you're wearing the costume, and you pass out your business card and you have all the bravado, you get respect. People do things for you. When you become a mom, it's a whole different world. Everyone treats you as a *mom*. And the thing I always come back to is— regardless of what I'm doing—I'm still me, dammit!"

Right, I say, just because she doesn't have the business card anymore, it doesn't mean she no longer has a head.

"I still have a head," Sharon confirms. "It's just not as valued." Not by litigators, anyway. That's the choice she made— to be more valued by her kids, maybe her husband, the school community. It's a perfectly good choice, but it is what it is.

Her lawyerly attention to detail and her professionalism have served her well in her new role. "There are a lot of things I love about being a stay-at-home mom," Sharon says. "If the school needs me to help decorate for Halloween, which is a blast, I love being able to say, 'Sure, I can do that.' I chaired the first-grade community service project this year, which was a great deal of fun for me. And I had the time to go put up posters for two hours. And I can go to chapel every Friday"—part of her daughter's school curriculum—"with her and see what she sees, and share that experience with her. And spend time with her one-on-one right after school when we walk home, just before we pick up her brother. We can talk about what's going on in her life and what she's doing, and I really value that. I value having an intimate relationship with them now."

As I listen, I wonder, *Do I have an intimate relationship with my kids?* I know what she's saying about leisurely strolls with your daughter after school, the soupçons of wonder and doubt they'll share only when they're alone, and in motion, with you, and the joy kids feel, seeing you among the open-armed mothers at that fabled school juncture, "pick-up." Would my kids and I be closer if I had the two hours now and then to put up posters at school?

I have noted how it agitates my children if, when I come home from work, I don't immediately change into "play clothes," as we call them, sweats or pjs—instead, reading mail and checking their homework while still in my regulation black and hard shoes. "Mommy, are you going out tonight?" they ask, anxiously. They worry about the world beyond our home that regularly lures me away.

I think back to when I was three or four years old in Brooklyn Heights, spending my days with Florence while my mother was off at work. I have this vivid memory of us being in front of some municipal building with a long flight of shallow stone steps full of working people, hurrying up and down. And suddenly I caught sight of some black pumps and nylon-clad calves, scissoring purposefully—and thought they belonged to my mother. I can still remember the sensation of Florence holding me back as I tried to rush toward the iconic-looking gams that belonged to a total stranger. But that busy image meant "mother" to me. Is it the same for my kids? Is their idea of me most vividly expressed by the back of a long black coat?

They know I love my job—a fact I've actually used against them when they misbehave. "You kids better cut it out," I'll say, home not five minutes, "or I'm turning right around and going back to work." Big eyes, silence, tense momentary calm.

Being a mom with a career does have its outlaw moments. In the current era, she may well answer to a different last name than the one used by her husband and kids. How profoundly weird, that quirk of our times. And yet I am not comfortable with the alternatives. I cannot get past the impression I sometimes have of the once-plugged-in working women I've known who give it all up for the children, suddenly finding themselves housebound, living by different lights entirely. When I witness their new routine and think about their lives now, the word that always comes up for me is *marooned*.

My sister never gave in to full-time child care; as a result she has been frustrated by the fragmented, on-and-off nature of her career. This has caused years of low-grade tension between us. (Wondering aloud about what I should get Hy for Christmas one year, my sister snapped, "I wouldn't know. I've never had a *Hy*.") I suspect she thinks I've got a cushy deal, although I'm sure she wonders what it has cost my children. And so do I sometimes. She can sew costumes for school plays, and her kids (and the entire school community) love her for it. At her house I find myself reading the birthday and Mother's Day cards pinned to the bulletin boards in which her kids extravagantly extol their mom's virtues; I scan them anxiously for references to traits I lack. Any mention of the making of costumes or "being there when we get home from school" brings me down for days.

I and my kind do the best we can, and our sweaty efforts often fall short. On my son's final day of preschool, it occurred to me that this was the last chance for him to enjoy the in-class birthday ritual and wear the paper crown, given that his actual birthday fell after school ended, and this particular group was about to disperse forever. As I'd barely learned the names of the other mothers and had already missed a slew of class outings, it seemed incredibly important to me that I not blow this event.

The problem was I had a 10 a.m. meeting and zero opportunity to whip up some birthday treats. So I called a stay-at-home mom friend in the neighborhood to ask where I could score something sweet on short notice. Nonsense, she said, she had the time and the ingredients; she'd take care of it. I objected; she insisted.

A few hours later, when I lifted the lid on the large, festive box to reveal two-dozen gorgeously decorated chocolate cupcakes, it was gratifying to hear the kids ooh and aah. But later, when one sugar-spiked, icing-smeared child called out, "Who made these?" it was with something less than pride that I heard my son call back, "My *mom.*" And no, I didn't correct him.

You dread that cruel rhetoric: if you only see your kids a couple of hours a day—that is, if you don't have time to make the cupcakes—why did you have the kids in the first place?

The newspapers are obsessed with the topic, and the headlines can put you to your knees: "Study Links Working Mothers to Slower Learning," said the *New York Times* a few years back. I cringed at the large-type pull quote: "*A baby with a mother who works is a toddler with farther to go.*" Another *Times* headline from July 2006 blared: "Two Studies Link Child Care to Behavior Problems." Then there are the incessant front-page stories about families making the Herculean effort to actually eat together once a week—stories about the curse of the oversubscribed child and the misbegotten, character-warping, future-stunting machinations of his equally oversubscribed parents.

There are also stories in the paper we take in bug-eyed and devour like pulp fiction, about the secret lives and nefarious influences of nannies: stories of joy-riding nannies, thieving nannies, IQ-lowering nannies, baby-shaking nannies, drug courier nannies, molesters, killers, fire starters, ghouls. You can practically hear the spit takes across the city as parents scan the headlines at the breakfast table over coffee.

And yet I've made the choices I have made because those couple of hours a day (plus entire weekends) I do see my kids are delicious, as soul-feeding and character-defining as work could ever hope to be. When things are going well, those two sides of my nature feed each other—and everyone in the family, I like to believe. During one atypical phase last year, I had to fly to Los Angeles three times over a six-week period, and I worried about the toll it was taking on the kids. But once I got home the third and final time, I was buoyed immeasurably by a drawing my then five-year-old son had made while I was gone. It was a cheerful, essentially thumbs-up drawing of a lady and a plane, with the headline, "The Advenchers of Mi Mom." Not bad, I thought. (At least it didn't say, "Mi Mom, The Sellfissh Absunty Bich.")

It's the life of my choosing, one in which I never have to do that tricky looking thing: ask my husband for money. I'll make my own, thanks. It's the life that I believe works the best for all of us. I have a friend in a similar boat whom I worship for expressing it so well: "I have a wonderful life. But I'm the architect of it."

The best mothers, working or not, go out of their way to respect the choices each of us has made, and to provide a sisterly assist wherever possible, refusing to take up arms in the so-called mommy wars. Consider my stay-at-home mom friend Lori ("stay-at-home" being a laughable misnomer in her case; she's on the run all day, doing for her family). She finds the most artful ways to remind me, without embarrassing me, about the form I might have forgotten to fill out or the project I have yet to volunteer for at the school. She knows what I'm up against and she's got my back.

Sharon is similarly generous. "So many working mothers are so hard on themselves, as if somehow they've failed, or disappointed their children," she says. "But I think having a life of your own is just one of the millions of steps you take every day toward making your children independent. It starts with playdates, which are a leap of faith"—that is, turning your kid over to strangers for an afternoon: " 'I'm trusting you with my most valuable thing. And I hope you treasure it as much as I do. Or at least don't throw a big truck at it.' "

I ask Sharon if she could ever imagine going back to work, if the idea of some relief from child care sounds at all appealing. She says she's contemplated it, although I can't be entirely sure if she's joking when she says she's even considered medical school. At least, Sharon says, it would promise long stretches when she wasn't in any way accessible to the kids. "So I could say, 'From one to three on Monday, Wednesday, and Friday, Mommy's got lab. On Tuesday and Thursday from two to four, Mommy's got lecture. Can't do anything about that!'" she chirps, sardonically. But medical school will have to wait. Not long after our conversation, Sharon became pregnant with kid number three.

You make your choices, the ones that are right for you. And if grace and good fortune are on your side, you embrace them. Failing that, do what I do and channel Popeye. "I yam what I yam," you must tell yourself, repeatedly.

THE GREAT BEYOND

T HE CALL COMES late at night. It's Debra, she's breathless. Something terrible has happened.

Mouth close to the receiver so the children won't hear—in tone and intensity, it's the sort of call you expect to get when your friend's marriage is breaking up. And in a way, that's what is happening. "Lucy," Debra says, "Ginger's leaving us."

Track the dynamic between mothers and the nannies they employ long enough, and you are bound to witness the phases and contours and emotional sweep that are characteristic of all full-blown relationships, romantic and not. In some cases, an initial, wary tentativeness is burnished by love and time into something smoothly routinized and mutually satisfying, born of a trust that was earned over the long haul. In other cases, giddy infatuation is ground down by the hardships of daily life and neglect. Attention isn't paid, feelings are hurt, love dies. Or more simply, people change. In the realm of child care, as the mother matures from neophyte into pro and the children go from helpless blobs into young adults, the all-knowing nanny might lose some of her mystique, her raison d'être in the household.

Whatever precipitates it, no matter how long you've known her, the end is always shocking. Early on, when we had to employ a temporary nanny named Kim for a few weeks while Hy attended an ailing parent back home, I felt what could only be described as paroxysms of grief when her time was up. I was moved beyond all description by the way Kim had stepped in so capably and helped us out during this raw, desperate period. By way of thanks, I got her a pair of leather gloves. And as I handed Kim the gift-wrapped box, I broke into sobs—the heaving, uncontrollable kind—as she helplessly, bemusedly looked on (recalling it, I don't think she was all that surprised by the display; she was a veteran in this game and had a feel for what I was going through). The whole thing was so intense, like a short-lived but fiery affair and its aftermath. Although I was thrilled that Hy would be coming back full-time, I could not face the fact that we'd never be seeing this other woman again.

LIFE INTRUDES

Several years ago, when Debra and I first started huddling to discuss our young children with such pleasure, and talk about these wonderful women in our lives—our nannies—our conversations brimmed with revelations, excitement, and awwww-inspiring anecdotes; anyone listening in could be forgiven for thinking we were talking about our crushes and first dates.

She described Ginger as the perfect person, a godsend. But as the girls' school day grew longer, the drift set in. And it was Ginger who pulled the plug.

She put it to Debra in a way that left little room for discussion: basically, she'd found a better situation elsewhere.

"In the last few days it was so hard," Debra says. "Ginger was clearly wanting to alleviate some of her . . . not guilt, but she wanted me to understand that her leaving was for a good reason. She'd say it wasn't me, it wasn't my children. But rather, she had found herself a good deal."

Did that in any way soften the blow? In detailing the extras and benefits of the new job—including better pay—she made Debra feel not only abandoned, but also lousy about everything she wasn't able to do for Ginger. "Again, I don't know what her motivation was, but the dynamic was so similar to a boyfriend that I was still in love with telling me that he still cared about me but he'd fallen in love with someone else, and she's even more beautiful than me, and she's a great cook, and don't you understand that I had to leave you? That was the feeling."

Another mother describes the moment the nanny resigns this way: "It's like being kicked in the stomach so many times. Because you think that this person . . . I mean they *do* love your children. But you think they're never going to leave you and that this is their first priority. But when it comes down to it, it's just a job. And that hurts like you cannot believe. They're taking care of your most precious possessions, and how can someone turn so quickly and just say, 'I'm going in two weeks?' It's unbelievable."

Yes, it's a horrible feeling, and my heart goes out to the mother who said this. But I can't help thinking back to a day a couple of years before, shortly after she'd had her second child. I asked her how the nanny was handling all the new responsibilities, now double what they were, in essence. The mom said fine, except for the fact that the nanny had asked for a raise because of all the extra work, and, well, they really didn't have the dough right now, so she had to tell her no. And as she's saying this, I'm distracted by the glow of her expensive blonde highlights, the glare of her diamond stud earrings. Could she really not afford the standard raise any nanny should be able to expect when there's suddenly a second child in the picture? This mother is neither cheap nor mean, and her nanny might have been out the door regardless. But I suspect her momentary negligence cost her.

Not only is the end of the line hard, but it sometimes can be unexpectedly messy as well. Ginger had been so important to the family that Debra badly wanted a ceremonious parting, including gifts and a celebratory night out. "Her last day was on a Tuesday, so on Thursday I'd said, 'We really want to take you out to dinner and thank you for six and a half of the most wonderful years, and for being the most incredible second mother to our children,'" Debra recalls. "And Ginger said, 'Well, let me see if I'm available.'" Debra pauses, still hurt by the memory of it. "I said, 'Whenever you're available we'll do it. Maybe you can find some time on Friday? Could you slot us into your calendar?' And she said, 'Maybe Tuesday.'

"So Tuesday afternoon I called her from work and said, 'Okay, at 6:00 I'll be home and we'll go right out to Sarabeth's. And there was silence, and I felt this kind of strange feeling. I said, 'Are you still up for this?' She said, 'Um, let me think about it.' I said, 'Okay, Ginger, listen. If you have to think about it, let's just forget it.' And she said, 'No, it's okay, I'll go.' And I said, 'Ginger, don't do me any favors.'

"So I got home and it was raining; I'd had a hard day at work and I said, 'Don't worry about dinner tonight, really.' But I still had to go get her cash, to pay her. So I took the kids out with me and Ginger, and I went to the bank to withdraw money. In the rain. And it was a very tense, painful, horrible, awful ending." On top of everything, Debra had assumed Ginger would leave her kids with a memento, be it a small gift or a note, something from her they'd have forever. But there was nothing. "I was crushed."

Debra had to wonder if she'd overestimated their closeness, if the relationship had been utterly one-sided. It haunted her to think Ginger was just hell-bent on getting the last dollar she was owed and moving on. What a relief it was to realize this wasn't the case.

"That weekend," Debra says, "she called me crying and told me that she misses the girls and loves them as if they were her own, and she doesn't understand what happened. It was all a miscommunication; of course she wanted to go to dinner with us, which was great for me to hear. Because honestly, when everything went down that day, I almost felt abandoned. But clearly it was a misunderstanding. I don't think I'm kidding myself when I say I know she cares about the girls deeply and will be part of their lives for a long time."

Debra has employed other sitters since, the first being Ginger's niece Arlene, twenty-five years old, who came with no experience. The first day she showed up, she was wearing six-inch heels, slacks in which she could neither squat nor bend over, and a midriff-baring shirt that revealed a pierced belly button. "She looked," says Debra, "like a living Bratz doll: she had big reddish-brownish-blondish hair, pillow lips, tons of cat-eye makeup—and a heart of gold." In a way, Arlene, so different in affect from the motherly Ginger, signaled the end of an era for the family, and the start of a new chapter in child care, given how much their needs were changing.

"I was so heartbroken when Ginger left," Debra says, "but now my girls don't necessarily require that strong maternal presence in a nanny. Now I guess I don't feel as though someone who takes care of them has to love them in that way. I did think that with Ginger, whom I had hired to be my surrogate— let's face it, that's what she was. But it doesn't really matter anymore, as long as the person is keeping them safe. They're taking care of my kids for three hours between school and the time I get home; they really only have to like them and enjoy them and have fun with them." Arlene left within a year to work as a hairdresser; now Debra's got a young woman who takes cheerful, efficient care of the girls with minimal emotional investment, and everyone's fine with it.

And to some extent Debra's still got Ginger, too, who calls, visits, and checks on the girls. Just like she said she would.

"It hit me like a ton of bricks," Marlene tells me, about being informed by her babysitter, Eva, that she was quitting her job to go on to nursing school. "I have never been more undone. I couldn't do my work. It took over my life, because I was just so worried about my children."

She reconstructs the moment. "It was the beginning of the day. She brings 'the paper' "—meaning some sort of official-looking document that explains a medical condition, a sickness in the family that the babysitter must go deal with, the new job she landed, or the program she's been accepted into. "That's happened to me so many times with nannies," Marlene says. "It's so typical: 'Here is the paper.' I'm like, don't give me the paper! But they want you to understand that everything's legitimate." With any luck, it quells the mother's shock and anger.

"She's a smart girl," Marlene says of Eva. "She's in her early thirties, and I realize there's more out there for her, and I don't hold that against her. But just be honest with me. Because what happened was, she set me up with her friend"—recommended her, assured Marlene she'd work out—"and she was terrible." Proffering the paper, offering up a friend, sometimes a nanny needs an exit strategy.

Many a nanny wants something a little better for herself, something with real benefits and job security. Others simply burn out on a job that is as emotionally demanding as it can be physically taxing.

"I think Joyce got a little bitter the last couple of years," Colleen says of the woman who nannied her children well into elementary school. Joyce was a paragon of good sense and efficiency at the outset; I can easily recall Colleen's impassioned testimonials during the first year. By the end, she'd grown ridiculously strict and short-tempered. "One time I just kind of said to her, 'What's going on here?' And she admitted to me she should have been in the army. She would have been a nun in the old days, she's so rigid. You could never be changing plans; if she had something in mind for the children and they wanted to go to the park, she could never, ever, ever change course.

"Around October the kids were getting very upset, saying Joyce was being mean to them. I'd come home at least two nights a week and they'd be crying." A charter member of the clean-plate club, Joyce would force the kids to eat every last crumb, and berate them for reading when they should be brushing their teeth. Then a number of mothers at school told Colleen that Joyce was being shockingly abrasive with her daughter, Emily. One day her son's temper tantrum pushed Joyce over the edge; she went running out of the house and down the street.

The problem was, Colleen couldn't bring herself to fire

Joyce. "I knew it was time for a change, but I also knew in my heart that I wanted it to end well," she says. But Colleen got incredibly lucky. Joyce, who was engaged, informed her one day that she wouldn't be returning to the job once she was married.

"When I told the kids that she was leaving, Emily, of all people, burst into tears and said, 'I would choose Joyce over any babysitter in the world!'" Colleen remembers, with a snort. "I think she had Stockholm syndrome."

THE VELVETEEN NANNY

"She must know it's coming. I mean, they all must know that," as one mother puts it, referring to the inevitable endgame of a job that's about caring for children. That difficult reality tends to overshadow even the strongest mother-nanny relationships. You turned to them when you and the baby were helpless. Suddenly nobody's so helpless anymore. The kids are growing lanky and sullen, they're no longer so easily diverted, and when they need encouragement, they turn to their peers.

The job is changing, dwindling, and everyone can feel it. The children have no end of afternoon commitments; often they're not even home until after six. They're even getting to the age where they can stay at home by themselves. The things you valued most in your nanny during those desperate early days, the subverbal ministrations to a little one for whom you had no aspirations greater than that it somehow stay alive, have fallen into disuse, irrelevance. And depending on the education and opportunities your nanny did or didn't have access to when she was young, the horribly awkward time may come when the children's abilities—to read, write, and play certain kinds of games—are eclipsing her own.

"Marta was so good when they were babies," says Maggie, the mother of eight-year-old twins in Houston. "She would take them on these hour-and-a-half walks in the park, where there was a big pond. She'd bring stale tortillas to our house, and every day they'd go feed the ducks. My son's first word was 'duck.'" Maggie pauses. "It's sad. When they got to be four or five and my daughter was reading . . . I don't think Marta reads that well. But she's sweet as could be.

"I started noticing when my kids went to school, they no longer were as enamored of her. It used to be on Monday mornings they'd scream, 'Marta! Marta! Marta!' and hug her and kiss her. Now when I pick them up from school on Fridays"—the one full day Marta still works for the family—"and drive them home, I say, 'Now remember to give Marta a hug and tell her you're glad to see her.' So now they walk in the house and dutifully go, 'Hi Marta, are you having a nice week?' And they hug her and go off and do their own thing. So"—and I literally flinch when Maggie says this—"she's like a piece of furniture.

"She doesn't do things with them anymore. In the summer we have a college girl, and she's fabulous. We were remodeling the bathroom and all the tiles came out, and she had the kids painting tiles every day. She wants to be a Montessori teacher, so she experiments on my kids. And I'm gonna have this beautiful garden with painted tiles someday."

I ask Maggie if the end is in sight with Marta. A silence. Then: "How do I say this? She doesn't want to leave, because she's been with us seven years. I'm just gonna let it die a natural death. One day she'll come in and say, 'Listen, I got a five-day-a-week job' and that will be it. It makes me sad, because she's been such a part of my kids' lives, and I'd hate for her to just disappear."

Now that the time has long since passed when the nanny can help with homework, that tutor will cost you extra. In terms of entertainment, those lazy afternoons in the park aren't going to cut it anymore; now music lessons and gymnastics will be competing for your family's leisure dollar and occupying your kid while the nanny's still on the clock. Constantly, compulsively, you do the math. Occasional babysitting: one hundred dollars a week. Tutor: eighty dollars a week. Music lessons: fifty dollars a week. Summer camp: three thousand dollars a year (and the school sports are pretty much free). Altogether, still not as much as you pay the nanny. When you find yourself donning the accountant's shade and firing up the adding machine in your brain several times a day, you know things can't stay the way they are for long.

Every hopeful effort is made to stave off the unthinkable: with her duties shrinking, the nanny says she no longer needs an annual raise. Furthermore, the hours can be adjusted; she can come in a few hours later and stay a concomitant few hours at the end of the day so that she's more available during the troublesome shank of the evening, when the help is most needed. As a new model for the job, this makes sense for a little while.

But the inevitable is hard to ignore. "Maybe," the mom suggests, "we could find you a morning job with someone who has a new baby, who just needs a few hours out of the house every day. Or maybe if you picked up a couple of house-cleaning jobs that you could do before coming to us . . ."

But the creative solutions fall flat. The nannies have heard them all before; they've tried those cobbled-together arrangements with other families and they know they never work, aren't worth the hassle. When you have two bosses, from time to time one or the other will be left tapping her feet and looking at her watch. And two families aren't likely to sync up their vacation schedules, leaving the nanny with no real time off. So the mom makes up some effusive, desperate flyers advertising her nanny's unrivaled services, and tacks them up on the pediatrician's bulletin board, the message board in the park, next to the ads for Pilates classes and used bikes.

Denise Landry, owner of a nanny agency, recommends a degree of straightforward realism from the start. She tells me about a nanny who, in any job she took, told it like it was to her charge when he reached the age of two or two and a half. "Out in the park or walking down the street she'd say to him, 'You know, that person drives a bus, that man looks after the park, that one takes care of sick people, and I'm a nanny. This is my job, because I love children. And when you're big, I might need to leave you and take another job, because you'll be in school.' That, I think, is important," Landry says. "It's a really nice way of saying this is not a permanent relationship."

But still, the end can be wrenching on everyone's part. Almost a decade ago, when I checked Hy's references, the father I'd spoken to about her for more than an hour on the phone summed up his feelings by telling me how hard he cried the day she left. Hy leaving—God, I can only imagine.

"That's what's so fascinating about it," playwright Lisa Loomer says. "It is a job and it's not, because it's about love. Part of the job requirement is to love. And sometimes when the relationship ends, I've known nannies who have become very depressed, because they miss the child. They feel the loss of a child. The nanny can feel jealousy when the mother takes over, and sometimes the children are jealous when they see the nanny with a new child."

"What would happen to me, may I ask, if I loved all the children I had to say good-bye to?" Mary Poppins says to the two freckle-faced kids in her care. One imagines there isn't a conflicted mother of young children alive who hasn't had that experience of watching the Disney movie—the one she saw a dozen times as a child for the chimney sweep dance and the weird animated interlude—and suddenly realizing that the pastel-hued, tuneful romp is a serious indictment of distracted mothers with ambitions beyond the home. Wry, overtaxed, financial wiz Kate Reddy, in *I Don't Know How She Does It*, is stunned to note the rendering of the pampered unmaternal mother as a foolish suffragette, fighting for women's rights at her kids' expense. Then there are the haunting, kill-me-now lyrics sung by all-knowing Bert the chimney sweep, about childhood slipping *"like sand through a sieve"*; the kids grow up, leave home, *"and it's too late for you to give."* Mary Poppins is only there to hold things together and help bring the parents around to the point where she's no longer necessary.

In real life, very rarely are the partings so clear-cut, providing blessed closure. Brenda left a family she loved and had been working with on Long Island for seven happy years before deciding she had to find a job with a less brutal commute. The comparatively simple matter of logistics was enough to undo this idyllic setup. "It was hard," she says, of saying goodbye to the boy and girl she'd taken care of so long and so well. "I walked away and I was crying. I said to them, 'I will always be checking on you.' And I did. I went to see them." She wipes her eyes with a paper napkin in the Manhattan diner where we chose to meet, her burger and fries growing cold. "It's making me emotional to talk about it."

You have been through so much together. You've been there for each other, you've each made the other's life possible. When May had to have some fibroids surgically removed, it was her boss, Joanne, who researched the operation on the Internet, interviewed doctors, and sorted through the insurance red tape. On the day of the operation, she took May to the hospital—she was the only one with her that day. "It was surprising when I woke up and she was there," May says. "Then she went home and got the boys and brought them back to see me. She made it all happen.

"Anything that I want I just have to ask her, and she finds a way of helping. When my father died, she helped me to go home by going on the Internet and finding the cheapest flights. She said, 'Stay as long as you want.' On my birthday she gave me two tickets to go see *On Golden Pond* with James Earl Jones. I took my nephew, and I laughed until my cheeks hurt. And I thought, this is the best present anyone could ever give me. My first real, live thing. She's great, she is the best. She has helped me out so much. I don't care what it is, she just has to ask me and I'll do it."

Of course, May has helped out Joanne heroically, too, having been there for the boys for more than a decade and seen the family through when the parents split up. Now she pings back and forth between their two apartments a few times a week. She's the only one of the lot who knows where to find the backpacks and books, the right sneakers, on any given day.

The problem is, Joanne's boys are getting big. The job is starting to shift. "Ben doesn't even want me to come get him from school now," May says of the middle-school-age boy, the younger of two. "When I come he says, 'What are you doing here?' and 'Oh, can you take my bag home? Bye!'—just like that, before running off with his friends. And yes, it hurts sometimes. Because to me, he's still my baby."

She describes how really upsetting it was the first time he

basically sent her away when she'd come to pick him up at school and accompany him on a playdate as she always had in the past. "I had already fixed dinner; there was nothing else to go home to do. I didn't want to just sit there and watch television. And so I stood there"—at the entrance of the school, where he'd dismissed her—"for like fifteen minutes." Eventually, his older brother showed up and in princely fashion, surely noticing her distress, asked May to come to the park with *him*—not that he needed a chaperone at his age. She was grateful. As a result, she says, "I didn't have to go home and cry over Ben not wanting me."

She has an apartment in the Bronx, but she lives with the family Monday through Friday, at one apartment or the other. Through the years, she has been the one to give the children their dinner, sit with them, and ask them about their day. As she puts it, "My life is really here. There is no boyfriend, there are no kids. I usually tell Ben I have two favorite days: Monday and Friday. I say, 'I love Monday because I know I have a job to go to. And Friday, I know you guys have to pay me!'" She laughs. "And he usually gets a kick out of that."

"Ben tells me I'm gonna be here until he goes off to college," May says. "So I'm hoping they'll need me until then."

SHOULD SHE STAY OR SHOULD SHE GO?

Some nannies are fired as cleanly and summarily as the shipping clerk who screws up one order too many. Helen finally dismissed her nanny when she realized she questioned the nanny's judgment. "For example," Helen says, "she frequently went on personal errands and took my son with her. And on one such errand, she nearly got into a fender bender with an elderly woman. In addition to yelling, 'Lady, what the F are you doing?' in front of my son, she also told him that 'old people shouldn't be allowed to drive,' which he happily repeated to us at the dinner table that night.

"She also said negative things about overweight people in front of him—she referred to one of the moms at his school as 'that really heavy woman'—and I just couldn't have that kind of prejudice seeping into my children's sensibilities this way, you know what I mean? I don't believe in describing people by physical characteristics anyway, like 'that black guy' or whatever. This is something I feel really strongly about, and stuff like this was what eventually led me to be a stay-at-home mom. Once children reach an impressionable age, you really do have to start worrying not just about whether or not a nanny is meeting their practical needs but also about her character, and what she may be teaching your child."

Still others leave or are phased out organically as the family itself grows into something else, sheds skin. And you ward off the tragic implications of making a break by suggesting you all remain friends, just as once-romantic couples sometimes do when they reach the end of the road. But the request that she return for a birthday party or dinner or an evening with the kids can be confusing. *Are you asking me to be your friend in my spare time, or is this babysitting?* the nanny wonders. Will money change hands?

It's a complicated, draining relationship, and those who've known it from the inside do not take it lightly, even after finding their way out. Abby, the former nanny from South Carolina who is now in publishing, was so cheerful and incessantly smiling during our conversation about the very nice family she worked for in Los Angeles, it surprised me when she finally rendered her judgment on the whole arrangement.

"I don't know if I could do it," she says when I ask her if she'd hire a nanny when it came time to have kids of her own. "I definitely wouldn't have a live-in nanny, probably because that was *me*. I loved the intimacy of my own family of four, growing up. And sometimes I felt like I was intruding on that with the other family. I don't know that I'd want someone else to be a part of that."

But for others there is no ambivalance. Elena, the first-time mother at forty-three, still berates herself for having been so anxious and high-maintenance in that first year with Sean. With regret, she tells me about feeling crowded by Gabriella, especially when Elena was breast-feeding her son, an experience she found to be transporting, sacrosanct. "I loved it," she says, "and who knew if I'd be able to still do it when I went back to work. So I was especially clinging to these moments. And I remember I'd sit on this couch, and Gabriella would stand behind it and wave at Sean, trying to get his attention while I was feeding him, and I would be so furious inside. I think it fed into my fear that she was going to steal his affection. It was like, This is *my* moment and *my* baby. Which is horrible."

And then Elena stuns me, suddenly choking up, growing inconsolable. "And let me tell you that the day she left, my husband and I and Gabriella wept for hours. She was the greatest nanny of all time." Unfortunately, she needed more hours than Elena could provide, on top of which she had moved, making her commute to their house intolerably long. "So it's kind of ironic that there I was those first weeks, this mother hen, like, 'get away from me,' and in the end I couldn't live without her."

I ask Elena how it was for her son when Gabriella left, right around the time he began his first year of full-time school. "He wasn't doing well," she says, composing herself. "He was acting out. He had a hard September. And just yesterday"— almost two years later—"we were driving, and out of the blue he said, 'Why did Gabriella leave when I went to school?'" Had he linked the trauma of Gabriella's departure with the trouble he was having? Or did Gabriella's leaving cause it?

Happily for all concerned, their families now celebrate holidays together; it's an unambiguous ritual that everyone enjoys. To this day, Elena and Gabriella talk on the phone regularly. Both have moved on to other child-care situations, perfectly acceptable, but nowhere near as deep or rewarding as what they had together.

"I'd do anything for her," one suburban New York mother says about her nanny. "I've given her five-thousand-dollar advances. I don't feel like I could live without her *personality* in my life every day, and I know she couldn't find a job equal to this. So I've weighed it: maybe if we have a third kid, we can stretch it out for more time. I know it's crazy. I don't want a third kid! And it really won't be an issue for a while, but being insane, I start projecting six years into the future."

In some cases it is impossible to say good-bye, and so you don't. Leslie has no intention of going through life without Patricia in her corner, despite the fact that her three boys are teenagers now; one just left for college, and the other two frequently don't roll home until dinner. "She's not going to get another job," Leslie says. "She wants to grow old with us. She works less and less every day—she doesn't come in until two o'clock now, and she gets us through dinner and then she goes home. But that's okay, because I need it.

"There are moods, like the day you walk in and she's just sitting there, unhappy, unrelated to anything in our life, but she has her own pressures. I always inquire: 'How do you feel?' because she's sick a lot. I've helped her out with her husband's illnesses; I've lent her money. I mean I want her life to be better, and she appreciates it. I love her and she loves us." In their case, till death do them part.

"Miss Lucy: With both kids in school, what's gonna happen this fall?"

It was the conversation I'd been avoiding. But Hy, forethoughtful and experienced in these matters, knew to bring it up. Our son was entering kindergarten, so technically speaking, the job as we knew it, which used to go nonstop from 8:30 a.m. until 6:30 p.m., now wouldn't begin until well past noon. Was this the beginning of the end? Her even raising the issue stopped me cold.

I thought back to Florence. We were so enmeshed with her that when we moved to Connecticut, she and my parents worked out some strenuous, misbegotten arrangement wherein she commuted to us from New Jersey three days a week. After less than two years of this, her husband put his foot down; presumably whatever my parents were paying her wasn't worth all that time apart.

We visited back and forth once or twice after that, but the relationship dissipated. Recently, I tried—and failed—to find a phone number for Florence. The last one we had for her was thirty years old. She'd be in her eighties now, if she is still alive.

I suggested the usual to Hy. Maybe if she got a morning job taking care of a baby, with a new mom who needs just a couple of hours, then came to us when it was time to pick up the kids from school . . . "But Miss Lucy, what if one of the kids is sick and I have to be here all day? I can't be taking care of a baby in the morning." Well, maybe if she got a cleaning job or two that she could do while our kids were at school . . .

Hy's dyspeptic look said it all; it felt wrong even suggesting it. She didn't need that back-breaking complement to whatever it was we'd be asking of her, just so we could save a little money. We agreed we'd all think on it.

Maybe a month later Hy brought it up again. As it happened, she'd been offered a full-time job taking care of a new baby, and if we were planning to cut her hours, she thought she'd better take it, even though she would prefer to stay with us.

The job isn't what it used to be. The children have piano and homework and playdates and tae kwon do. Their worlds are getting bigger. That said, there is still plenty to do—no end of schlepping and kid-corralling. Besides . . .

It was Hy who bathed the kids in the blue plastic tub, and fed them farina from a rubber-coated spoon. It was Hy who laughed with me as we wedged a pudgy, clueless Sophie into a clown costume for her first Halloween (and Owen into the same costume three years later). It was Hy who painted Sophie's tiny toenails for the first time, and Hy who held newborn Owen in the hospital—the first to do so after my husband and me (and a couple of nurses). It was Hy who comforted the kids when I was on the rampage—or late, or absent; Hy who brought them stuffed dogs wearing crocheted Rasta hats when she returned from a hard-earned week in Jamaica. On cold days, it was Hy who called to remind us to dress the kids warmly, and Hy who, every night, let them climb her like a pole, wrap their legs around her waist, and paste her with kisses, until she settled them down with that one hopeful word: "Tomorrow."

So yes, we are sticking with Hy. Because for now—maybe forever—she is family.

ACKNOWLEDGMENTS

A heartfelt thank you to all the mothers and nannies who so generously shared their stories with me. I am also grateful to the passionate Karen Rinaldi and the meticulous Kathy Belden from Bloomsbury for their help and care throughout. Many thanks also to my gifted agent, Bill Clegg, and to Ai-jen Poo of Domestic Workers United for years of invaluable consultation.

I have had two amazing bosses during the writing of this book, *GQ* editor-in-chief Jim Nelson and *Marie Claire* editor-in-chief Joanna Coles, and I am indebted to both for their inspiration and support. In truth I couldn't make a move without my formidable near-and-dears Anne Bergeron, Lisa Henricksson, Thomas Mallon, and Elizabeth M. Welch; love and thanks to each of them. For their unwavering faith in me I say thank you to my parents, Peggy and Walter Kaylin, to my wonderful sister, Jennifer, and her family. To Kimball, Sophie, and Owen, how lucky I am to be making my life with you. And to Hy, thanks indeed. For everything.

A NOTE ON THE AUTHOR

LUCY KAYLIN is the executive editor of *Marie Claire*. She was a features editor at *GQ* and is the author of *For the Love of God*. She lives in New York with her husband and two children.